Mastering
the
MICROWAVE

Over 150 mouthwatering recipes

Ann Page-Wood

Hodder & Stoughton
LONDON SYDNEY AUCKLAND

For information about the Weight Watchers classes, contact: Weight Watchers UK Ltd, Kidwells Park House, Kidwells Park Drive, Maidenhead, Berks SL6 8YT. Telephone (0628) 777077

Art Director: Lawrence Back
Photography: Simon Smith
assisted by Thierry Guinovart
Home Economist: Ann Page-Wood
Styling: Kathy Man

British Library Cataloguing in Publication Data
Page-Wood, Ann
    Mastering the microwave.
    I. Title   II. Weight Watchers
    641.7

ISBN 0-340-59322-9

Published by Hodder and Stoughton,
a division of Hodder and Stoughton Ltd,
Mill Road, Dunton Green, Sevenoaks,
Kent TN13 2YA
Editorial Office: 47 Bedford Square,
London WC1B 3DP

Photoset by SX Composing Ltd, Rayleigh, Essex

Printed in Great Britain by BPCC Hazell Books Ltd, Aylesbury, Bucks.

Microwave on front cover by kind permission of Panasonic Consumer Electronics UK

The publishers would like to thank Toshiba (UK) Ltd and Panasonic Consumer Electronics UK for use of microwave ovens.

Contents

INTRODUCTION

This book has been written for everyone interested in microwave cooking. Microwaves have transformed the age-old methods of cooking in just a few years. Since the 1950s when the microwave was introduced into this country its popularity has steadily increased and now a microwave oven is considered an integral part of the modern kitchen. The microwave has many advantages. It can be used to speed-up traditional methods of cooking, reduce preparation time, and cook extremely quickly. It retains the flavour and texture of many foods, makes efficient use of fuel, and reduces the amount of cooking utensils and therefore cuts down on washing-up. However, some people give up using their microwave as an 'oven' and use it purely to thaw or reheat food. Although a microwave oven does have limitations, in the same way a conventional oven has, it can be used successfully when the basic techniques have been mastered.

It is easy to forget the early mistakes we all made when learning to cook with a conventional oven and it's easy to feel defeated after one or two microwave failures. Although practice and perseverance will lead to successful cooking it is important to understand what microwaves are, the variety of ovens and power levels, how they cook food, and which containers aid microwave cooking. For this reason the first section of this book explains some of these basic facts. The following chapters are devoted to particular foods and includes facts relevant to their cooking as well as recipes which can be simply and successfully prepared in the microwave. The last section answers questions frequently asked about microwaves.

About Microwave Cooking

WHAT ARE MICROWAVES?

Microwaves cannot be seen, they are similar to the waves which carry radio and television signals from transmitter to receiver. These waves are high frequency and their length is extremely small – hence their name 'micro' waves.

HOW A MICROWAVE OVEN COOKS FOOD

When a microwave oven is turned on the electricity voltage passes to a magnetron. The magnetron converts the electrical energy to microwave energy and the microwaves are channelled to a 'stirrer' which stirs the waves fairly evenly into the oven chamber. Just as radio waves have particular properties, the way microwaves are transmitted, reflected and absorbed determines their character. The metal walls of the oven and the mesh in the door deflect the waves and they bounce from one wall to another and from top to bottom in a criss-cross pattern.

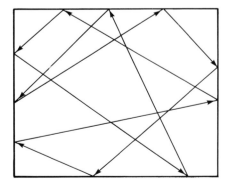

Microwaves pass through microwave cookware but are attracted by the water and fat molecules in food. The waves penetrate 1½ – 2 inches (4-5.5cm) of the food and agitate the molecules at high speed, millions of times per second, causing heat by friction. This can be understood by rubbing hands together. When hands are rubbed against each other they become warm and the faster they are rubbed the quicker they warm up. As the molecules in the food vibrate their heat is conducted to areas where the waves do not penetrate – the areas beyond 1½ – 2 inches (4-5.5cm). When the oven door is opened or when the microwave oven is switched off the production immediately stops. The oven does not alter temperature. This is completely different from the conventional method of cooking. When a conventional oven is switched on heat is generated and conducted throughout the chamber and even after the oven is turned off it remains warm for some time.

CONTAINERS

'Microwave-safe' containers are made from materials which allow microwaves to pass through them and enable the waves to be absorbed by food. These materials include paper, china, pottery and oven-proof glass. Materials which reflect the microwaves, like metals, are not suitable. Metal ties such as those which are used to tie plastic bags and the foil wrapped round confectionery must never be used in a microwave oven.

Only extremely small pieces of aluminium foil can be used, and even then they have to be completely smooth, with the shiny side facing the food. Aluminium foil must never touch any part of the oven. It can be very useful when cooking foods which contain bones or have particularly thin or delicate areas, fish for example. If tiny pieces of foil are carefully laid over the head and tail they will deflect the waves.

As foil and metals cause the waves to be deflected a blue spark is sometimes produced, this is called arcing. If arcing occurs the oven must be immediately turned off as the spark will damage the magnetron. If any sparks appear when you use foil to shield small parts of the food it is sensible to stop using it altogether.

To test whether a container is safe to use in the microwave pour 5fl oz (150ml) of water into it and place in the oven. Set the oven to HIGH and cook for 1 minute 30 seconds. If the water is hot and the container cool it should be microwave-safe, however, if the container is hot and the water cool it must not be used in the oven.

The following list gives information about materials which can be safely used for cooking or reheating food in a microwave oven.

Paper
Unwaxed paper plates may be used in the microwave oven. Paper kitchen towels are useful as moist foods can be rested on them to absorb some moisture, for example when cooking jacket potatoes. Greaseproof paper, non-stick baking parchment and paper doyleys can also be laid underneath food which is to be served directly from the oven. However, these are not suitable if the food is moist. Avoid using patterned paper, it may colour the food.

Plastic
Plastics suitable for microwave cooking are usually labelled 'microwave-safe' but even these tend to discolour after a while. Plastic lids usually have small vents to allow steam to escape and they are manufactured in sizes that will fit over most dishes. Yogurt pots are unsuitable but some thin plastic containers and freezer bags may be used for very short periods to thaw food. They are not suitable for cooking as the heat from the food causes them to melt. Microwave clingfilm and roasting bags are useful but check the labels to make sure they are microwave-safe. Clingfilm makes an ideal covering for bowls or dishes but it should not be in contact with food. When clingfilm is required to cover food, for example fish which should be cooked flat, either use a shallow dish or a plate with a raised edge so the clingfilm does not rest on the fish. Pierce a few holes in the film or pull a corner back to prevent it ballooning up during cooking.

China, Pottery and Glass
Most types of china, pottery and oven-proof glass can safely be used in the microwave. Food can therefore be cooked and served in attractive dishes. Delicate china and china decorated with metal, even if just the manufacturer's name is written on the base in metal, are unsuitable. Thick china and pottery absorb a small amount of the microwaves and so the cooking time would have to be lengthened. Ovenproof glass can be used in the oven but thin or delicate glass containers can easily shatter as the temperature of the food increases. Never place cut or leaded glass in a microwave oven.

Wood
Wooden bowls may be used when reheating rolls prior to serving, but as they tend to dry out and crack their use is limited. Wooden spoons and spatulas may be rubbed frequently with a small amount of oil to prolong their life but do not use excessive amounts of oil or they will generate heat.

Wicker Baskets

These should be used in the same way as wooden containers but always check to make sure they do not contain metal staples or glue which causes arcing or melting.

Fabrics

Pure cotton napkins may be used to line baskets containing bread or rolls which are to be warmed before serving but check the fabric is 100 percent cotton, man-made fabrics should never be placed in the microwave.

The size and shape of a container is important. Containers should be large enough to hold food in a single layer and not cause spillage. Recipes containing a high proportion of liquid must have sufficient room for the liquid to boil without overflowing. Meat, fish, fruit and vegetables should be placed in a single layer so the microwaves can cook them evenly. Whenever possible square and rectangular dishes should be avoided as the microwaves penetrate the first 1½-2 inches (4-5.5cm) and consequently become more concentrated in the corners. This resulsts in food overcooking in the corners yet remaining cool in the centre.

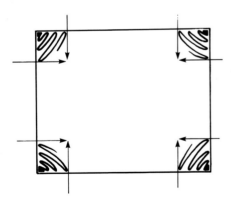

Bowls or round-bottomed containers or containers with sloping sides are not desirable for general use because the waves tend to accumulate around the base. The ideal shape would be a round, straight-sided dish with a slightly concave base. These containers are not available

at present so substitute a round dish with straight sides and a flat base. This shape will enable the waves to be absorbed from the base, top and outer edge.

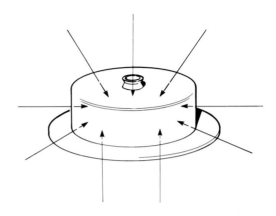

A ring-shaped dish works well since it allows the waves to reach the food from the top, bottom and inner as well as the outer edge of the circle. However, this is obviously unsuitable for recipes which require stirring during cooking. A glass or cup can be placed in the centre of a round dish to create a space thus enabling the waves to penetrate from the middle to the outer edge.

When two or more containers are placed in the oven at the same time they should be placed apart and off centre. Even when an oven is fitted with a turntable food may need rearranging during cooking. It is an advantage to use a microwave-safe trivet or roasting rack to raise food to enable the microwaves to penetrate more easily from the base, but if you don't possess one an upturned plate or saucer may be substituted.

MICROWAVE ACCESSORIES

Many accessories are now manufactured for the microwave. These include containers and clingfilm already mentioned but I am defining 'accessory' as an item which would aid cooking but is not absolutely necessary for basic cooking.

Browning Dishes

These dishes are the only containers which can be placed in the oven on their own without any food. They are designed to absorb microwave energy and therefore heat up and act in the same way as a grill or frying pan. They have to be heated for a short while, usually 4-8 minutes, before food is placed on them. When the first batch of food has been seared or cooked the dish requires heating once again as the food absorbs the heat and consequently the dish cools. Always follow the manufacturer's instructions. Oven gloves should be used when handling browning dishes as they become extremely hot. Dishes which have a browning base should always be heated without the lid.

Thermometers

Never use conventional thermometers in a microwave oven. They may be inserted in food which has been removed from the oven but never use them at any time during cooking. Specially designed microwave thermometers are useful accessories particularly when cooking meat or making jams, but always follow the manufacturer's instructions.

Microwave-safe Roasting Racks and Trivets

These are useful for cooking meat as they allow the juices and fat to drip out and away from the meat. They can also be used as a rack for supporting dishes such as ring moulds or circular cake containers. The cake is then raised from the oven base so the microwaves have easier

access to the base of the container and the mixture is nearer to the top of the oven where the waves tend to be stronger. This results in more even cooking.

Plate Rings

These are useful for reheating two plates of food simultaneously as one can be stacked on top of the other. They are not a very good way of heating three or more plates of food as the one in the centre does not heat up as quickly as the others.

MICROWAVE OVENS AND FEATURES

There are many different types of microwaves on the market, some have one power level and a low wattage, others have a number of settings, up to nine, and a variety of features. Choosing a microwave oven can be bewildering. It is important to understand the basic differences between the ovens before deciding which one will suit your particular needs.

Many factors influence the choice of oven: it must be large enough to cook the quantities of food you or your family require, fit comfortably in the space where it is to operate, and, if it is to be built into a kitchen, a suitable model should be bought since many have air vents at the side or top. If you decide to have a microwave oven built above a conventional oven the manufacturer's instructions should be carefully studied as they usually advise at least 6 inches (15cm) between the two. Cost is obviously an important consideration and recently ovens have come down in price but don't be misled, the cheaper models are usually less powerful than the more expensive ovens. There is not a wide choice of colour, most models are brown or white, but there are a few other colours being introduced and a grey and white design is already available. All microwave ovens should carry the B.E.A.B. (British Electrotechnical Approvals Board) safety mark.

WATTAGE AND POWER LEVELS

The oven's wattage determines the power output. Until September 1990 there was no standard method of determining the output of an oven. All members of the

Association of Manufacturers of Domestic Electrical Appliances (AMDEA) have now agreed to conform to the International Electrotechnical Community (IEC) standard number 705. The wattage is determined by a given test: one litre of water must be heated for a specified time on the highest setting of an oven which has been standing at room temperature. If you own an oven which was bought prior to September 1990 I suggest you contact the manufacturer to find its IEC wattage. The higher the wattage the faster the food will cook. For example, an 800 watt oven on HIGH power would cook twice as quickly as a 400 watt oven set at its highest power level. Ovens of the same wattage will differ from one another as factors such as the size of the oven chamber affect its performance. The power varies by up to 8 percent, when there is a surge of power a 650 watt oven could be cooking at about 700 watt and when the power decreases the same oven on the same setting could be cooking at 600 watt.

Ovens have many different power levels, some have only one output while others have up to nine different settings. This variation makes recipe instructions difficult to express. The models with nine settings give an opportunity to cook food nearest its optimum temperature. The settings usually express the power, for example, the setting '5' refers to 50 percent power which would mean a 650 watt oven would then be cooking at 325 watts. Some ovens have five power levels: HIGH, MEDIUM HIGH, MEDIUM, MEDIUM LOW and LOW. These express the power of the oven from 100 percent to 75 percent, 50 percent, 30 percent to the lowest setting 10 percent.

The recipes in this book were tested in a 750 watt (IEC − previously 650 watt) oven using three settings HIGH − 100 percent power, MEDIUM − 50 percent power and LOW − 30 percent power. Although this doesn't allow for the great variation many people are fortunate enough to have, it does enable the majority of microwave owners to make use of the recipes and so gain confidence to make up their own recipes and adapt old favourites. Always refer to the manufacturer's instruction book to determine the wattage and power levels. If your oven is not 750 watt (IEC) use these times as a guide.

550 watt (IEC) add 20 seconds per minute
850 watt (IEC) deduct 10 seconds per minute.

AUTOMATIC PROGRAMMING
Ovens fitted with an automatic programme facility can set the oven to cook on more than one power setting. For example, cooking may start on HIGH then be reduced to a lower power for the remaining cooking time. This facility may be useful to set the oven to thaw food at a low setting and then increase the power to re-heat.

TEMPERATURE PROBE
This facility is offered with some ovens. It controls cooking by registering the internal temperature of the food. The probe must be inserted into the food, usually a joint of meat, at its thickest part and not touching any bone, then it is plugged into its special socket within the oven chamber and the desired temperature given in the manufactuer's instructions is set. The power is automatically switched off when that temperature has been reached.

ADVANTAGES OF A MICROWAVE OVEN
I consider a microwave oven a time-saving appliance which not only cooks food efficiently but also retains many flavours and textures that are altered by conventional methods of cooking. However, I do not consider microwave ovens an alternative to the traditional cooker. Both methods of cooking are valuable and each have their particular advantages.

Some recipes, such as Yorkshire Puddings, cannot be made successfully in the microwave oven; they do not rise, turn golden brown, nor do they have the recognisable crisp texture. Deep fat frying should never be attempted in a microwave oven, though this is hardly a disadvantage as the health conscious will recognise. On the other hand a microwave oven is very versatile, cooks food extremely quickly, and cuts down the amount of fat required to cook foods such as stir-fried vegetables. It combines a number of processes and can be used to thaw, reheat, poach, stir-fry, bake, roast, boil and steam food. It can speed-up considerably the preparation of food and hastens processes such as the proving time for bread.

It is often claimed that a microwave oven can be considered an economical method of cooking but, although it is undoubtedly true that cooking times are frequently reduced, sometimes by up to one-quarter, some processes would not be undertaken without a microwave. Frozen food for example would normally be left to thaw at room temperature. Fuel is saved when a small quantity of food is to be cooked, as a microwave oven starts to cook food immediately the oven is switched on. A considerable amount of fuel is used just to heat up a conventional oven.

A microwave oven makes it possible to thaw food, reheat and serve it from the same dish. Small quantities of food can be reheated with little loss of texture and it is therefore ideal for families which have different eating times. The meal can be served on a plate, covered and then reheated when required. Most ovens are fairly small and they can be moved from one place to another with little effort. They are also an asset to the disabled because, as the oven doesn't heat up, there is little chance of being burned accidentally, and the visually handicapped, as well as many other disabled people, are able to cook more easily.

Conventional processes are used to aid microwave cooking just as microwave cooking can improve traditional methods. Some examples of the combination of methods can be seen when an electric kettle boils water quickly and economically for use in a microwave oven, and a traditional grill browns and gives crispness to microwaved recipes. The microwave oven cooks a jacket potato in a few minutes but the skin remains moist. By transferring cooked potato to a hot grill the moist skin dries and becomes crisp – the best of both worlds!

A Summary of Microwave Techniques

TEMPERATURE
The temperature of food will affect the cooking time: food taken from the refrigerator will take longer to cook than food stored at room temperature.

SHAPE
The shape of both the food and the container will affect time and evenness of cooking; a boned and rolled joint of meat will cook more evenly than one still on the bone. Whenever possible cut food into even-sized pieces and use containers which are round with straight sides and that are large enough to hold the food in a single layer. A shallow dish will enable food to cook more quickly than a deep container. Allow plenty of room for liquids to boil, and never fill more than two-thirds full. Arrange food in a circular pattern with the thicker or denser end nearer the outer edge.

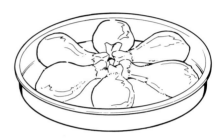

Chicken drumsticks – thinner end towards the centre as the thicker end, which contains more meat, requires more cooking

STIRRING AND REARRANGING
During cooking stir food frequently or rearrange by turning food 90 or 180 degrees. This is sometimes necessary even when an oven is fitted with a turntable. If an item is more than 2½ inches (7.5cm) thick turn over halfway through the cooking time as the microwaves tend to be stronger at the top of the oven.

DENSITY
A food which is denser than another will take longer to cook or thaw. For example a piece of French bread will take less time to thaw than the same weight of an ordinary loaf because its texture is lighter.

QUANTITY
The more food in the oven the longer the cooking time, conversely the less food the less the cooking time. When adapting recipes use the following as a guide: half the quantity of food will take half to two-thirds the cooking time, but double the quantity

Broccoli florets – stalk to outer edge of dish otherwise the florets will overcook

will take about an additional one-third to half the time. Use a container that suits the amended recipe and decrease or increase the standing time.

SHIELDING

Food which is uneven in shape may require shielding. Small quantities of foil – which must not touch any part of the oven – may be used to shield chicken wings, fish tails etc but it may be possible to arrange some food so that this is unnecessary. For example, fish fillets may be arranged with the thinner tails overlapping in the centre.

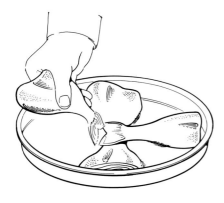

Lay fish fillets in a round dish with the tails slightly overlapping in the centre

PIERCING

Food encased in a skin must be pierced or slit to avoid it bursting or exploding. Pierce the skins of vegetables such as potatoes and aubergines. Eggs should be shelled and then the yolk very carefully pierced with a wooden cocktail stick.

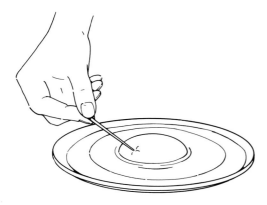

COVERING

Food which is moist will require covering during cooking but food which requires a dry texture, for example a cake or a loaf, should remain uncovered. Either cover containers with a lid or use pierced clingfilm. Always remove the covering with extreme care to prevent scalds. Lift the edge of the lid or clingfilm furthest away from you then draw it back on itself.

Pierce or slit roasting bags and either pierce clingfilm or leave just under a quarter of the dish uncovered if the mixture is to be stirred during cooking.

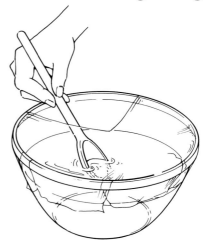

STANDING

If in doubt always undercook food, if necessary it can always be returned to the oven. Allow standing time so cooking can be completed by the conduction of heat within the food. Fruit and vegetables require very short standing times but, by leaving them to stand for a minute or two, overcooking is avoided. A few minutes are necessary to complete the cooking of rice, as it is during the standing time that its cooking liquid is absorbed. Longer times are essential for large items such as roast joints. The temperature of meat can increase by 5-10°C during the standing time. During this period the meat should be covered with foil to retain its heat.

ADAPTING RECIPES
Avoid the use of salt, it draws moisture from the food. As food is generally cooked much quicker in a microwave oven some desirable flavours don't have time to develop. It may be preferable to make a casserole the day before it is to be served then reheat when required, alternatively seasoning can be adjusted after cooking but prior to serving. Reduce the amount of liquid in recipes such as soups and stews by about one-third but increase the quantity of liquid in a cake to give a slacker mixture. As very little browning takes place while food is cooking a browning agent may be suitable for enhancing its appearance. Some recipes, such as a potato topping or the crust of a loaf, can be browned under a grill.

Meat

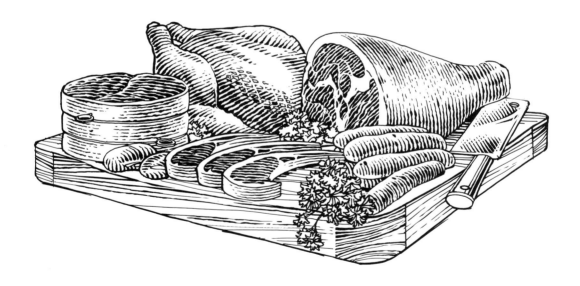

Tender cuts of meat and poultry are suitable for microwave cooking. Tough cuts require tenderising before cooking and even when the meat is cut into very small cubes and cooked on LOW for a long time the meat doesn't compare favourably with traditional casseroling or pressure cooking.

Choose good quality meat. Beef should be deep red with a small amount of creamy marbling of fat. Pork pale pink with only a slight marbling of fat and a slight pink tinge to the bones. Lamb and veal pinky red in colour, there should be no deep red patches. Bacon should be a deep pinky brown colour. Salted bacon is unsuitable as it turns brittle during cooking. An indication that poultry is fresh is an evenly-coloured skin and a well-rounded body. Never buy meat which has been resting in its own juices or smells unpleasant.

Store meat carefully. Remove the covering and transfer to a plate, cover and keep in the refrigerator. Cook minced meat, sausages, offal and poultry as soon as possible, preferably on the day purchased. Other meat may be stored for one or two days. Allow meat to reach room temperature before cooking.

When purchased, frozen meat and poultry should be wrapped in a completely airtight container and it should be of good even colour. Always thaw before cooking, this can be carried out in the microwave but the manufacturer's instructions must always be followed carefully to ensure even thawing. There must be a standing time to allow this process to be completed.

Fat is extremely high in calories and therefore as much of the visible fat as possible should be trimmed off before cooking. A proportion of the invisible fat in beef, pork, lamb and bacon can be removed by three methods.

1. Lay the meat on the rack of a conventional grill and cook, turning once, until the fat stops dripping.

2. Place the meat on the microwave roasting rack, lay a piece of greaseproofpaper over it and cook for a short time as recommended in the recipe, until the fat stops dripping.

3. Pour sufficient liquid over the meat to just cover then cook until boiling, cool rapidly and skim the fat from the surface.

Always roast meat on a microwave-safe roasting rack or trivet. If you don't have one an upturned plate or saucer may be used, so it isn't resting in its own juices. Remove poultry skin before serving; a layer of fat is stored directly beneath the skin. The following recipes list the weight of uncooked meat which has been trimmed of all fat.

CASSEROLING
Only high-quality tender meat can be successfully casseroled in a microwave oven. The dish should be covered and stirred from time to time. Cuts of beef usually purchased for grilling, for example rump steak, are suitable but other meats take a long time and would be better cooked by traditional methods.

MICROWAVE 'GRILLING'
Although the microwave doesn't grill food by direct heat I have used this term to distinguish between the small cuts of meat which would be conventionaly grilled from joints which are traditionally roasted. Steaks, chops, offal, chicken and even minced meat can be microwave-grilled.

Offal, veal and skinned chicken may be microwave-grilled but, as they dry out quickly, brush well with oil or cook by other methods such as in casseroles or in split roasting bags.

Lean beef, lamb, pork and ham require little preparation. Trim all visible fat from the meat and then place on a microwave-safe roasting rack or trivet. Minced meat should be shaped into balls or burgers then laid on the rack. A piece of greaseproof paper must be laid over the meat to prevent the remaining fat spitting over the oven. Avoid the use of paper towels as they tend to stick to the meat. I sometimes lay a piece of kitchen paper in the trivet to prevent fat spitting but this is not essential. Unlike traditional grilling the meat will not turn golden brown during cooking so it may be desirable to sprinkle over a little microwave browning agent. Some of these browning agents contain a lot of salt so it is better to shake them over the meat only a short while before the end of the cooking time. Sausages look particularly strange if they are not coloured. Although a browning dish could be used for browning meat it is not suitable for anyone wishing to follow the recommendations for a healthy diet and reduce their consumption of fat. The fat would be sealed in the meat and in some cases, when additional oil is required to coat the dish, the total fat content would increase.

ROASTING

Meat which is boned, rolled and even in shape is the most desirable joint for roasting but this is not always possible. Joints with a bone, for example leg of lamb, can be roasted but the bone should be shielded with a small piece of smooth foil securely held in place with a wooden cocktail stick. Whole chickens have to be trussed into a good or well-rounded shape then the tips of the wings and breast bone shielded with a little foil.

To roast meat: place fat side down on a trivet resting over a plate then cover with the trivet top, or a split roasting bag. Turn the meat 180 degrees halfway through cooking and pour off any of the juices and fat which drip into the base of the dish. This is important as fat attracts microwaves and they would be directed to the trivet not the meat. Large joints should be turned 90 degrees three or four times during cooking. If a rare finish is desired, omit turning but continue to remove the fat and juices.

Chicken should be cooked breast side down for the first half of the cooking time then turned over for the cooking to be completed.

Standing time is essential for all roasted joints, allow about 5 minutes per pound (450g). During this time the temperature of the meat will rise about 5°C. Cover the joint on the roasting rack with a tent of foil, so that the foil encases the joint.

Opinions differ regarding the power levels for roasting, some recommend HIGH, others LOW. I have tried both but find there is very little to choose between them therefore I consider cooking on HIGH power for a shorter time preferable.

The following times are to be considered a guide for roasting, but remember that the temperature of the meat as well as the shape of the joint and the amount of bone affects cooking times. Remove the joint from the refrigerator 1-2 hours before cooking so it reaches room temperature. Always weigh meat which is stuffed after stuffing, before calculating the cooking time. If you prefer meat rare or well done decrease or increase the cooking times accordingly. For very accurate results it is well worth investing in a special microwave thermometer. The meat can then be removed from the oven about 5°C lower than the recommended temperature after standing. A conventional meat thermometer should otherwise be inserted into the meat, when it has been removed from the microwave, to check the correct temperature has been reached.

	Setting	Minutes per per lb (450g)	Temperature after standing
Beef:			
rare	HIGH	7 minutes	60°C
medium	HIGH	8 minutes	70°C
well-done	HIGH	8½-9 minutes	75°C
Lamb	HIGH	9 minutes	80°C
Pork	HIGH	10 minutes	80°C
Veal	HIGH	9 minutes	75°C
Chicken	HIGH	8 minutes	90°C

Roast Sirloin

3lb (1.4kg) sirloin

1. Check the weight of the joint and allow 8 minutes per pound (450g). Insert the microwave thermometer and place the joint on a microwave roasting rack resting on the roasting dish. Cover with the rack hood or lay a split roasting bag over the joint and tuck under the beef so the fat can easily be drained during cooking.

2. Cook the joint on HIGH for 10 minutes, carefully remove from the oven and either spoon the fat and juices from the dish or transfer the rack to another plate.

Tip out the fat and juices then replace the meat, turn 180 degrees then cover and return to the oven. Cook on HIGH for 7-8 minutes then remove the fat and juices from beneath the joint, cover and cook on HIGH for the remaining 6 minutes or until the thermometer registers 65°C.

3. Lift the joint from the rack and place on a large square of foil with the shiny side against the meat, wrap the foil round and leave to rest in a warm place for 15 minutes.

Selections per serving:
3oz (90g) cooked beef = 3 Protein Selections

Use the chart opposite as a guide for cooking times and settings but remember that the temperature of the meat, its shape, thickness and other factors will affect the cooking time. Whenever possible meat should be cooked from room temperature, not directly from storage in the refrigerator, and be of even size and shape. If the meat is ¾ inch (2cm) or more thick turn halfway through cooking. Undercook rather than overcook – it can always be returned to the microwave for a short time. Leave the meat to stand for 2-3 minutes before serving.

Cooking Guidelines for Meat

Meat & Weight	No. Of Servings	Protein selection per serving	Calories per Serving	Setting	Time	Additional instructions
chicken:						
1 × 4oz (120g) boned chicken breast	1	3	140	HIGH	2½-3 mins	Cover loosely with split roasting bag, thin ends towards centre.
2 × 4oz (120g) boned chicken breasts	2	3	140 each	HIGH	3½-4 mins	
4 × 4oz (120g) chicken drumsticks	4	2½	95 each	HIGH	8-9 mins	Pierce skin three of four times, cover loosely with split roasting bag. Turn once during cooking. Arrange with bone ends towards centre.
lamb:						
2 × 3oz (90g) best end loin chops	1	3	110 each	HIGH	3-3½ mins	Cover, turn once during cooking.
1 × 4oz (120g) chump chop	1	2¾	145	HIGH	3-3½ mins	
2 × 4oz (120g) chump chops	1	2¾	145 each	HIGH	4½-5 mins	
pork:						
1 × 3½oz (105g) loin chop	1	2½	140	HIGH	3-3½ mins	Cover, turn once during cooking.
2 × 3½oz (105g) loin chops	2	2½	140 each	HIGH	5-5½ mins	
2 × 3½oz (105g) loin chops-boned	2	3	165 each	HIGH	5½-6 mins	
bacon:						
1 × ½oz (15g) rasher back	1	1	65	HIGH	40-50 secs	Cover.
1 × 1oz (30g) rasher back	1	2	130	HIGH	1-1¼ mins	
beef:						
1 × 4½oz (135g) rump steak	1	3½	225	HIGH	2¼-2¾ mins	Cover, turn once during cooking.
2 × 4oz (120g) rump steak	1	3	200 each	HIGH	3½-3¾ mins	
sausages:						
2 × 1oz (30g) chipolatas	1	1½	200 each	HIGH	1½-1¾ mins	Pierce skin several times. Cover, turn once during cooking.
4 × 1oz (30g) chipolatas	1	3	200 each	HIGH	2-2½ mins	
1 × 1½oz (45g) sausage	1	1¼	150	HIGH	2-2½ mins	
2 × 1½oz (45g) sausages	1	2½	150 each	HIGH	2½-3 mins	
1 × 1¼oz (40g) frankfurter	1	1	110	HIGH	35-45 secs	Pierce several times, cover.
2 × 1¼oz (40g) frankfurters	1	2	110 each	HIGH	45-55 secs	

Crown Roast of Lamb

Serves 4
400 Calories per serving

A crown roast is usually fatty and not suitable for the health-conscious, but this method of preparation and cooking results in a lean succulent joint.

2 racks of lamb total weight about 2½lb (1.2kg), boned, not chined, cut between the bones

10oz (300g) carrots, cut into ½ inch (4cm) lengths

10oz (300g) courgettes, cut into ½ inch (4cm) lengths

1   Using a sharp knife remove the white fat from the back of the racks leaving just sufficient membrane to hold the ribs together. Tie the racks together with the chops outward.

2   Crumple a piece of greaseproof paper into a ball and place in the centre of the crown. Weigh the joint and calculate the cooking time, allowing 8 minutes per pound (450g).

3   Place the crown on a microwave roasting rack, cover with the roasting hood and cook on HIGH for half the calculated time. Remove the joint from the oven, tip out any juices in the dish under the rack, then turn the crown round 180 degrees. Cover and cook for the remaining cooking time.

4   Remove the greaseproof paper. Place the meat in a tent of foil and leave to stand allowing 5 minutes per pound (450g).

5   Place the carrots in a container, add 2 tablespoons of water, cover and cook on HIGH for 3 minutes. Add the courgettes, stir round then cover and cook on HIGH for 2 minutes 30 seconds.

6   Transfer the Crown Roast of Lamb to a plate, pile some of the cooked vegetables in the centre and serve the remainder separately. Serve with potatoes, gravy and mint sauce – calculate the additional Selections and calories as necessary.

Selections per serving:
3 Protein
1¾ Vegetable

Roast Stuffed Leg of Lamb

Serves 8
270 Calories per serving

It is important that the lamb is good quality, tender, without gristle. I prefer to buy from a butcher and not rely on the supermarket prewrapped joints. Serve half the lamb hot for four people, and the remainder as a cold meal, or freeze for future use.

1 boned leg of lamb, approximately 2¼lb (1.1kg)

for the stuffing:

3oz (90g) onion, finely chopped

½ medium red pepper, seeded and finely chopped

4-5 tablespoons chopped mint

1 small clove garlic, crushed

3oz (90g) fresh breadcrumbs

2 tablespoons skimmed milk

Selections per serving:
¼ Bread
3½ Protein
10 Optional Calories

1   Place the onion and red pepper in a bowl, cover and cook on HIGH for 2 minutes 30 seconds.

2   Stir the mint, garlic and breadcrumbs into the vegetables and add the milk to bind.

3   Spoon the stuffing into the leg, if necessary use your hand to ensure the stuffing is evenly distributed.

4   Roll up the stuffed leg and tie into a neat shape with string. Weigh the joint and calculate the cooking time allowing 10 minutes per pound (450g) – the time is longer than for cooking lamb joints on the bone.

5   Transfer the joint to a roasting rack, cover with the hood and cook on HIGH for half the cooking time. Remove the joint from the oven, tip out and reserve any of the meat juices from the dish beneath the rack. Turn the leg over and return to the oven. Cook on HIGH for the remaining cooking time.

6   Remove the Stuffed Leg of Lamb from the oven, place in a tent of foil and leave to stand, allowing 5 minutes per pound (450g). While the joint is standing cook the vegetables then skim the fat from the meat juices to make a gravy.

Lamb Curry

Serves 4
290 Calories per serving

Use a tender cut of lamb for this recipe, cheap stewing lamb is not suitable as there is not sufficient time for it to tenderise.

1lb (480g) lean lamb – leg or loin

8fl oz (240ml) stock or water

⅜ inch (1cm) slice ginger

1 clove garlic

1 onion

1 red pepper, seeded

2 teaspoons oil

1 teaspoon turmeric

½ teaspoon ground cinnamon

½ teaspoon ground cumin

1 teaspoon ground coriander

approximately ¾ teaspoon hot chilli powder

1oz (30g) flour

1 tablespoon tomato purée

½ medium mango

6oz (180g) frozen mixed vegetables

1　Cut the lamb into 1 inch (2.5cm) cubes, place in a suitable container and cover with the stock or water. Cover the container and cook on HIGH for 8 minutes. Leave the lamb in the stock to cool, then skim the fat from the surface of the stock.

2　Peel, then finely chop the ginger, garlic and onion. Chop the pepper.

3　Place the oil, ginger, garlic, onion, red pepper and all the spices in a bowl or container, stir round then cover and cook on HIGH for 5 minutes.

4　Stir the flour into the spicy mixture, add the tomato purée then gradually stir in the stock and lamb.

5　Cut the mango into ½ inch (1.25cm) cubes. Stir the mango and frozen mixed vegetables into the lamb mixture, cover and cook on HIGH for 16-18 minutes, stirring twice during cooking. Leave to stand for 5 minutes.

Selections per serving:
　¼ Bread
　½ Fat
　¼ Fruit
　3½ Protein
　1 Vegetable
　5 Optional Calories

Sweet and Sour Lamb

Serves 2
240 Calories per serving

Use good quality lean lamb for this recipe, there isn't sufficient time to tenderise the cheaper cuts.

2 × 4oz (120g) boned leg fillet of lamb

1 tablespoon cornflour

1 teaspoon tomato purée

1½ teaspoons vinegar

1½ teaspoons soy sauce

½ teaspoon sugar

1 tablespoon sweet sherry

6 tablespoons stock

½ medium onion

½ small red pepper, seeded

3oz (90g) tiny cauliflower florets

3oz (90g) drained canned sweetcorn

1½ oz (45g) sugar peas or mangetout

salt and pepper

1 Lay the lamb on a microwave rack, place a piece of kitchen paper under the rack and lay a piece of greaseproof paper over the meat. Cook on HIGH for 3 minutes 30 seconds.

2 Blend the cornflour, tomato purée, vinegar, soy sauce, sugar and sherry together with the stock.

3 Chop the onion and cut the pepper into ½ inch (1.25cm) squares.

4 Cut the lamb into 1 inch (2.5cm) cubes. Place the lamb, onion, pepper, cauliflower and sweetcorn into a container, stir in the blended tomato purée mixture.

5 Cover the Sweet and Sour Lamb and cook on HIGH for 4 minutes then stir and cook on MEDIUM for 5 minutes. Stir the sugar peas or mangetout into the container, cover and cook on MEDIUM for a further 1 minute 30 seconds. Leave to stand for 4 minutes, season with salt and pepper then serve.

Selections per serving:
  ½ Bread
  3 Protein
  1½ Vegetable
  30 Optional Calories

Sweet and Sour Lamb and Grapefruit Cup (see page 184)

Shepherd's Pie

Serves 2
400 Calories per serving

The cooked pie may be browned under a grill if desired.

8oz (240g) lean minced beef

4fl oz (120ml) stock

9oz (270g) potatoes

2oz (60g) onion

3oz (90g) mixture of carrot and swede

2oz (60g) frozen peas

1 tablespoon cornflour

2 teaspoons tomato purée

3 tablespoons skimmed milk

salt and pepper

Selections per serving:
  1½ Bread
  3 Protein
  1 Vegetable
  45 Optional Calories

1   Place the minced beef in a bowl, add the stock, cover and cook on HIGH for 4 minutes. Leave to cool – if you are in a hurry stand the bowl in cold water so the stock cools quickly – then skim off the fat which floats to the surface.

2   Slice the potatoes and place in a container, add 3 tablespoons water, cover and cook on HIGH for 4 minutes until cooked.

3   Finely chop the onion and dice the carrot and swede then place in a container, add 2 tablespoons of the minced beef stock, cover and cook on HIGH for 2 minutes 30 seconds. Remove from the oven and stir in the frozen peas.

4   Blend the cornflour together with the stock. Add the beef, tomato purée and carrot mixture then cover and cook on HIGH for 4 minutes, stirring halfway through the cooking time.

5   Drain the potatoes and mash together with the milk, season with salt and pepper. Spoon the cooked beef and vegetables into a small pie dish. Spoon the mashed potatoes on top and roughen the surface with a fork. Return to the oven and cook uncovered on MEDIUM for 5 minutes. Leave to stand 2-3 minutes.

Beef with Ginger

Serves 2
265 Calories per serving

The steak should be no more than ¾ inch (2cm) thick. If the meat is under ½ inch (1.25cm) thick the cooking time should be reduced a little.

2oz (60g) thin French or Kenyan beans

juice of half a medium orange

7oz (210g) rump steak

1 teaspoon oil

1½ teaspoons finely chopped ginger

1 clove garlic, finely chopped

2oz (60g) parsnip

2oz (60g) swede

2 tablespoons beef stock

Selections per serving:
  ¼ Bread
  ½ Fat
  ¼ Fruit
  2½ Protein
  ½ Vegetable

1 Top and tail the beans, cut them into 1½ inch (4cm) lengths and place in a container with the orange juice. Cover and cook on HIGH for 3 minutes or until cooked but a little crisp.

2 Cut the rump steak in half then lay on the microwave roasting rack or trivet. Lay a piece of greaseproof paper over the meat and cook on HIGH for 4 minutes. Remove the beef from the oven and leave to cool.

3 Place the oil, ginger and garlic in a container, cover and cook on HIGH for 45 seconds.

4 Cut the parsnip and swede into thin lengths the same size as the beans. Place the parsnip, swede and beef stock in the container with the garlic and ginger, cover and cook on HIGH for 4 minutes.

5 Stir the beans and orange juice into the parsnip mixture, cover and cook on HIGH for 1 minute.

6 Slice thinly across the width of the beef, it should still be a little pink in the centre. Transfer the beef to the hot vegetables, stir well then cover and cook on HIGH for 30 seconds.

Beef Casserole

Serves 4
280 Calories per serving

Use only good quality beef for any casseroles or stews to be cooked in a microwave oven, expensive roasting or grilling cuts are ideal but topside and brisket give a good flavour and cook well. I tested this recipe with a good quality blade and it worked well but required 50 minutes to become tender.

14oz (420g) braising steak

7fl oz (210ml) stock

2 teaspoons vinegar

1 large onion

9oz (270g) potatoes

10oz (300g) mixture of carrot and swede

2oz (60g) mushrooms

2 teaspoons flour

¼ teaspoon mixed herbs

salt and pepper

Selections per serving:
¾ Bread
3 Protein
1½ Vegetable
5 Optional Calories

1   Cut the beef into small pieces, ¾ inch (2cm) square. Place the beef in a dish, add the stock and vinegar then cover the dish and cook on HIGH for 6 minutes until boiling. Remove from the oven and set aside until cold and the fat has solidified on the top. Remove the fat.

2   Chop the onion. Cut the potatoes into large chunks, about 1½ inches (4cm) square. Slice the carrot and cut the swede into 1 inch (2.5cm) cubes. Roughly chop or halve the mushrooms – the different sized pieces of the vegetables are necessary to give fairly even cooking.

3   Place the onion in a dish, cover and cook on HIGH for 1 minute 30 seconds.

4   Add the potatoes, carrot and swede to the onion, stir in 3 tablespoons stock from the beef dish, cover and cook on HIGH for 5 minutes.

5   Sprinkle the flour over the vegetables then stir in the stock, beef, mushrooms and herbs. Cover the dish and cook on HIGH for 5 minutes, stir well then cook on LOW for 40-50 minutes or until the beef is tender. Leave to stand for 5 minutes, season with salt and pepper then serve.

Corned Beef Hash

Serves 2
430 Calories per serving

The cooked peas may be substituted with cooked diced carrots, swede or celeriac but remember to adjust the Selections and calories as necessary.

9oz (270g) cooked potatoes

1 small onion

2 teaspoons margarine

4oz (120g) corned beef

1 teaspoon tomato purée

½ teaspoon mustard

2 tablespoons skimmed milk

½ teaspoon Worcestershire sauce

2oz (60g) cooked peas

1 Cut the potato into ½ inch (1.25cm) dice.

2 Place the potatoes in a container, add 3 tablespoons water, cover and cook on HIGH for 4 minutes. Leave covered while preparing and cooking the other ingredients.

3 Finely chop the onion. Place the margarine and onion in a container, cover and cook on HIGH for 2 minutes.

4 Cut the corned beef into ½ inch (1.25cm) dice.

5 Blend the tomato purée together with the mustard, milk and the Worcestershire sauce.

6 Stir all the ingredients together, add the cooked peas, cover and cook on HIGH for 2 minutes 30 seconds. Stir once during the cooking time.

Selections per serving:
  1½ Bread
  1 Fat
  2 Protein
  ¼ Vegetable
  30 Optional Calories

Chilli Con Carne

Serves 2
355 Calories per serving

This dish is cooked uncovered for the last 2 minutes of the cooking time, this reduces the liquid and therefore concentrates the flavour. The amount of chilli may be increased or decreased according to taste.

8oz (240g) lean minced beef

8fl oz (240ml) stock

1 clove garlic

approximately ¾ green chilli

1 onion

1 teaspoon oil

2 teaspoons flour

good pinch mixed herbs

2 tablespoons tomato purée

6oz (180g) drained canned or freshly cooked kidney beans

1   Place the minced beef in a dish, pour over the stock so that it just covers the meat. Cover and cook on HIGH for 6 minutes, leave to cool then skim all the fat from the surface.

2   Finely chop the garlic and chilli. Chop the onion.

3   Place the oil, garlic, onion and chilli in a dish, cover and cook on HIGH for 3 minutes 30 seconds.

4   Sprinkle the flour into the onion and stir well then add the minced beef and stock, herbs, tomato purée and kidney beans.

5   Mix all the ingredients together and break up any lumps of beef.

6   Cover the dish and cook for 5 minutes, stirring halfway through the cooking time.

7   Stir the Chilli Con Carne well then continue cooking, uncovered for 2 minutes. Place a lid over the dish and leave to stand for 4 minutes.

Selections per serving:
   1 Bread
   ½ Fat
   3½ Protein
   ½ Vegetable
   20 Optional Calories

Veal with Lemon Sauce

Serves 2
255 Calories per serving

The rice which is to be served with this recipe may be cooked on the hob while the veal is cooking in the microwave. Frozen or freshly cooked rice may be covered and reheated in the microwave between stages 8 and 9 of the method.

3 tablespoons spring onions

4fl oz (120ml) skimmed milk

zest of ½ lemon, removed with a potato peeler

2 × 4oz (120g) veal escalopes

1 teaspoon margarine

1-2 teaspoons lemon juice

pepper

2 teaspoons cornflour

2 tablespoons single cream

9oz (180g) hot cooked rice

Selections per serving:
1½ Bread
½ Fat
3 Protein
80 Optional Calories

1 Place the spring onions, milk and lemon zest in a jug or bowl, cook on HIGH for 1 minute 30 seconds. Leave for 20-30 minutes to infuse.

2 Lay the veal escalopes between two sheets of damp greaseproof paper and, using a rolling pin or steak hammer, beat until very thin.

3 Grease a plate, large enough to hold the veal escalopes with ½ teaspoon margarine, use the remaining margarine to grease a sheet of greaseproof paper.

4 Lay the veal on the greased plate and sprinkle with the lemon juice, season with pepper and cover with the greased greaseproof paper, then tuck it under the meat.

5 Remove the lemon zest from the infused milk and gradually blend the milk together with the cornflour, stir in the cream.

6 Cook the sauce on HIGH for 2 minutes 30 seconds, stirring every 30-40 seconds, until boiling and thick.

7 Cook the veal on HIGH for 3 minutes, leave to stand for 2 minutes. Reheat the sauce for a few seconds if necessary.

8 Divide the hot rice between two serving plates, lay the veal on top of the rice and pour the sauce over.

Chicken in Watercress Sauce

Serves 4
265 Calories per serving

If possible buy a bunch of watercress for this recipe, it is more economical than the packets of sprigs and has coarser stalks which give a stronger flavour.

1½-1¾oz (45-55g) watercress

2 teaspoons margarine

2 tablespoons finely chopped spring onions

1oz (30g) cornflour

14fl oz (420ml) skimmed milk

6oz (180g) drained canned sweetcorn kernels

12oz (360g) cooked chicken

Selections per serving:
  ¾ Bread
  ½ Fat
  ¼ Milk
  3 Protein
  ¼ Vegetable
  10 Optional Calories

1 Reserve a few sprigs of watercress, chop the remainder and place in a container together with the margarine and spring onions. Cover and cook on HIGH for 1 minute 30 seconds.

2 Blend the cornflour to a smooth paste with 4 tablespoons milk. Heat the remaining milk on HIGH for 2 minutes.

3 Stir the hot milk into the cornflour paste, stirring all the time then pour into the watercress mixture and add the sweetcorn.

4 Cut the chicken into large chunks and stir into the watercress mixture.

5 Place the chicken mixture in the oven and cook, uncovered on HIGH for 7 minutes, stirring every 1 minute 30 seconds. Leave to stand for 4 minutes. Spoon the Chicken in Watercress Sauce into a serving bowl and garnish with the reserved sprigs of watercress.

Chicken in a Creamy Wine Sauce

Serves 4
200 Calories per serving

As the chicken and sauce are very pale I suggest the dish is served with a selection of brightly coloured vegetables.

2oz (60g) leek – white part only

4fl oz (120ml) white wine

4 × 4oz (120g) skinned boneless chicken breasts

1½ tablespoons cornflour

3 tablespoons single cream

salt and pepper

paprika

Selections per serving:
3 Protein
¼ Vegetable
75 Optional Calories

1   Chop the leek as finely as possible.

2   Place the leek and 3 tablespoons wine in a container, cover and microwave on HIGH for 1 minute 30 seconds.

3   Lay the chicken breasts in a large container with the thicker ends towards the edge of the dish and the thinner ends slightly overlapping in the centre. Pour the remaining wine together with the partially cooked leeks and wine over the chicken, cover then cook on HIGH for 6 minutes.

4   Blend the cornflour together with the cream.

5   When the chicken is cooked, carefully remove the breasts and leave to stand, covered, on a plate. Stir the cornflour mixture into the hot leeks and wine then cook, uncovered, on HIGH for 1 minute 30 seconds. Stir once during the cooking time. The sauce must be thick and the leeks completely cooked. Season with salt and pepper.

6   Transfer the chicken to four serving plates, spoon the sauce over and sprinkle over a little paprika.

Chicken Casserole

Serves 4
185 Calories per serving

Use this recipe as a basis for your own. The mangetout may be added at the same time as the chicken but they won't retain their crisp texture.

1 large onion

1 red pepper

3oz (90g) baby corn on the cob

2oz (60g) mushrooms

1oz (30g) mangetout

½ pint (300ml) chicken stock

1lb (480g) skinned boneless chicken breasts or thighs, or a mixture

1 tablespoon cornflour

¼ teaspoon tarragon

1 Thinly slice the onion. Remove the core and seeds from the red pepper and cut in half then cut each half into thin slices.

2 Keep the very small corn whole, cut the others in half.

3 Slice the mushrooms, top and tail the mangetout.

4 Place the onion and red pepper in a container, add 2 tablespoons stock then cover and cook on HIGH for 3 minutes 30 seconds.

5 Cut the chicken into 1½ inch (4cm) pieces, toss in the cornflour.

6 Stir the chicken and tarragon into the hot onion and pepper. Cover the container and cook on HIGH for 12 minutes, stirring twice during the cooking time.

7 Stir in the mangetout, cover and cook on HIGH for 2 minutes. Stand for 5 minutes.

Selections per serving:
  ¼ Bread
  3½ Protein
  1 Vegetable
  10 Optional Calories

Chicken Risotto

Serves 6
480 Calories per serving

Serve this dish with a mixed salad.

few grains of saffron

4 tablespoons warm water

2 × 1oz (30g) rashers lean back bacon, derinded

1 clove garlic

1 onion

1 red pepper

2 teaspoons oil

1lb (480g) skinned boneless chicken

3oz (90g) mushrooms

8oz (240g) long grain white rice

12fl oz (360ml) boiling chicken stock

salt

2 tablespoons chopped parsley

3oz (90g) drained canned sweetcorn

¼ large avocado (3oz/90g)

Selections per serving:
 1½ Bread
 ¾ Fat
 3 Protein
 1 Vegetable
 5 Optional Calories

1 Place the saffron in a small bowl, add the warm water and leave to infuse for 2-3 hours, or longer.

2 Lay the rashers of bacon on a microwave rack, place a piece of kitchen roll underneath and a piece of greaseproof paper over the bacon. Cook on HIGH for 50 seconds. Allow to cool then chop.

3 Finely chop the garlic. Chop the onion, remove the seeds from the pepper then cut into small dice.

4 Place the oil, onion and red pepper in a container, cover and cook on HIGH for 4 minutes 30 seconds.

5 Cut the chicken into pieces, about 1 inch (2.5cm) square.

6 Stir the chicken into the hot onion mixture, cover and cook on HIGH for 4 minutes, stirring halfway through the cooking time.

7 Slice button mushrooms or roughly chop flat mushrooms. Add the mushrooms, infused saffron, rice, boiling stock and a little salt to the chicken and vegetables. Add the parsley and sweetcorn then cover and cook on HIGH for 11 minutes, stir once halfway through the cooking time.

8 Roughly chop the avocado and stir into the hot risotto when the power is turned off. Cover and leave to stand for 6 minutes.

Kentish Pork

Serves 4
190 Calories per serving

This unusual dish is perfect for cooking in the microwave, the apples retain their shape and colour and the flavour of sage, apple and pork blend together well.

6oz (180g) lean minced pork

2 teaspoons finely chopped sage

1 tablespoon grated onion

2oz (60g) breadcrumbs

1 small egg, size 5

1oz (30g) hard cheese, grated

2 medium cooking apples

Selections per serving:
½ Bread
½ Fruit
1½ Protein

1   Mix the pork together with the sage and onion. Shape the pork mixture into four patties and lay on a roasting rack. Lay a sheet of kitchen paper on a plate then rest the roasting rack on top and cover with a piece of greaseproof paper.

2   Place the pork patties in the oven and cook on MEDIUM for 2 minutes or until the fat has stopped dripping from the pork. Leave to cool for 2-3 minutes.

3   Stir the breadcrumbs together with the egg and cheese. Crumble the pork patties into the breadcrumb mixture and mix well.

4   Peel the apples, cut in half and remove the cores. Arrange the four halves of apple in a circular pattern on a plate.

5   Divide the pork mixture into four. Shape each quarter of pork into a circle and press into each half of the apple. Make a criss-cross pattern on the pork then cover and cook on HIGH for 4 minutes. Leave to stand for 2 minutes then transfer to a serving plate.

Pork and Bean Supper

Serves 4
185 Calories per serving

Serve this dish with broccoli and cauliflower.

8oz (240g) lean pork, eg leg or tenderloin

1 small onion, chopped

½ green pepper, seeded and chopped

¼ pint (150ml) stock

¼ teaspoon mixed herbs

9oz (270g) baked beans in tomato sauce

6oz (180g) potato, grated

1 teaspoon Worcestershire sauce

1   Cut the pork into ½ inch (1.25cm) cubes.

2   Place the pork, onion, green pepper, stock and mixed herbs in a bowl, mix well then cover and cook on HIGH for 5 minutes. Allow to cool then skim off any fat that rises to the surface.

3   Stir the baked beans, potato and Worcestershire sauce into the pork mixture, stir well, cover and cook on HIGH for 6 minutes.

4   Stir well, then reduce the heat and cook on MEDIUM for 9-10 minutes until the potato is cooked and the meat tender.

5   Leave to stand for 4 minutes.

Selections per serving:
½ Bread
2¼ Protein
¼ Vegetable

Pork Ragoût

Serves 4
175 Calories per serving

If you prefer, fresh herbs may be used in place of dried; substitute ¼ teaspoon dried herbs with 1 teaspoon finely chopped fresh herbs.

4 × 3oz (90g) lean boneless pork chops

6oz (180g) leeks

½ small red pepper

½ small yellow pepper

6 tablespoons apple juice

¼ teaspoon mixed herbs or sage

½ medium dessert apple

salt and pepper

Selections per serving:
  ¼ Fruit
  2½ Protein
  ¾ Vegetable
  5 Optional Calories

1 Lay the pork chops on a microwave roasting rack, place a piece of kitchen paper under the rack and lay a piece of greaseproof paper over the top of the meat. Cook on HIGH for 3 minutes 30 seconds.

2 Thinly slice the leeks and cut the peppers into thin strips.

3 Place the prepared vegetables, 4 tablespoons apple juice and the herbs in a dish, cover and cook on HIGH for 4 minutes.

4 Peel and remove the core from the apple, cut into four slices.

5 Stir the remaining apple juice into the dish, lay the pork chops on top of the vegetables then arrange the apple slices over the chops.

6 Cover the dish and cook on HIGH for 2 minutes 30 seconds. Leave to stand 2 minutes then season to taste with salt and pepper.

Sausage Roll-Ups

Serves 4
75 Calories per serving

These sausages may be served on their own as a savoury to serve with drinks or they can be eaten with a vegetable or cheese dip.

4 × 1oz (30g) pork and beef chipolata sausages

OR 8 × ½oz (15g) pork and beef cocktail sausages

1oz (30g) lean back bacon, derinded

mustard

Selections per serving:
  1¼ Protein

1 Using a fork, pierce each sausage several times.

2 Lay the bacon flat on a work surface then spread the mustard thickly over the rasher.

3 Cut the bacon into four long thin strips, cut each strip in half.

4 Roll one strip loosely round each end of all the sausages or, if using cocktail sausages, roll the bacon loosely round each sausage. Secure the bacon with wooden cocktail sticks.

5 Lay the sausages on the rack of a microwave roasting rack or trivet. Lay a piece of kitchen paper under the trivet and a piece of greaseproof paper on top of the sausages. Cook on HIGH for 1 minute 30 seconds, turning once. Leave to stand 2 minutes. Cut each sausage in half and serve hot or cold.

Liver with Orange

Serves 2
245 Calories per serving

Liver is rich in iron, a substance required to help transport oxygen throughout the body. The combination of citrus fruit and liver aids the absorption of iron.

½ medium onion

3oz (90g) carrot

3oz (90g) swede

1 medium orange

1½ teaspoons tomato purée

7oz (210g) sliced lamb's liver

Selections per serving:
  ½ Fruit
  2½ Protein
  1½ Vegetable
  5 Optional Calories

1   Slice the onion and cut the carrot and swede into 1 inch (2.5cm) lengths about ¼ inch (5mm) thick.

2   Place the onion in a container, cover and cook on HIGH for 1 minute 30 seconds.

3   Cut the orange in half lengthways, squeeze the juice from one half and peel then roughly chop the remainder.

4   Stir the carrot, swede, orange juice and tomato purée into the onion, cover and cook on HIGH for 4 minutes.

5   Cut the liver into six then stir into the hot vegetables with the chopped orange. Cover and cook on HIGH for 3 minutes, stirring halfway through the cooking time. Stand for 2 minutes. The liver should be very slightly pink when cut through the centre, if it is not sufficiently cooked return to the oven and cook, covered, for a further 20-30 seconds.

Kidney Casserole

Serves 2
150 Calories per serving

This casserole is very simple to make. Don't cook the kidneys too long or they will be tough and rubbery.

½oz (15g) rasher lean back bacon, derinded

4 × 2oz (60g) lamb's kidneys

1 large leek

2oz (60g) button mushrooms

2 teaspoons margarine

3oz (90g) frozen mixed vegetables

2 teaspoons flour

1 teaspoon tomato purée

½ teaspoon mustard

1 tablespoon chopped parsley

6fl oz (180ml) stock

Selections per serving:
   1 Fat
   3½ Protein
   1½ Vegetable
   10 Optional Calories

1 Place the bacon on a microwave rack, cover with a piece of greaseproof paper and cook on HIGH for 40 seconds. Leave to cool then chop into small pieces.

2 Remove the skin from the kidneys, cut in half and remove the white central core – this is most easily done by snipping with a pair of kitchen scissors.

3 Thinly slice the leek and mushrooms.

4 Place the sliced leek and margarine in a container, cover and cook on HIGH for 1 minute 30 seconds.

5 Add the frozen mixed vegetables, cover and cook on HIGH for 1 minute 30 seconds – do not add any water.

6 Turn the kidneys in the flour.

7 Stir the tomato purée, mustard, 2 teaspoons parsley and stock into the sliced leek. Add the kidneys and mushrooms, stir round then cover and cook on HIGH for 7 minutes, stirring two or three times during the cooking time.

8 Leave to stand for 2-3 minutes. Sprinkle with the remaining parsley then serve.

Tripe and Vegetable Casserole

Serves 2
155 Calories per serving

This recipe makes a change from the traditional tripe and onions.

10oz (300g) dressed tripe

2 large onions

4 sticks celery

4fl oz (120ml) stock

4fl oz (120ml) tomato and vegetable juice

2 bay leaves

½ teaspoon marjoram

pepper sauce

salt

Selections per serving:
  ¼ Fruit
  3½ Protein
  2½ Vegetable

1 Cut the tripe into eight pieces.

2 Thinly slice the onions and celery, add 4 tablespoons stock, cover and cook on HIGH for 7 minutes.

3 Stir the tripe, remaining stock and the tomato and vegetable juice into the onion mixture.

4 Crumble the bay leaves and marjoram into the onions.

5 Add a dash of pepper sauce then cover and cook on HIGH for 4 minutes, stir once again, cover and cook on MEDIUM for 15 minutes.

6 Stand for 4 minutes then season with salt and add a little more pepper sauce to taste.

Simple Speedy Supper

Serves 1
305 Calories per serving

Short of time and don't feel like cooking?   This is when the microwave can really help. Follow the method below and a meal can be cooked in 5 minutes.

6oz (180g) baked beans in tomato sauce

½oz (15g) lean back bacon, derinded

2 × 1¼oz (40g) frankfurters

2oz (60g) mushrooms

1 tomato

Selections per serving:
  2 Bread
  3 Protein
  1½ Vegetable

1 Place the baked beans in a container, cover and cook on HIGH for 2 minutes, stir halfway through the cooking time. Leave covered while preparing the rest of the meal.

2 Lay the bacon and frankfurters on a microwave rack, cover with a piece of greaseproof paper and cook on HIGH for 1 minute 30 seconds or until the bacon and frankfurters are cooked.

3 Slice the mushrooms and halve the tomato. Place the mushrooms and tomato halves on a serving plate, cover with an upturned bowl and cook on HIGH for 1 minute 20 seconds.

4 Transfer the cooked bacon and frankfurters to the plate, spoon on the beans and serve.

Fish

Fish is particularly well suited to microwave cooking, it retains a good flavour, texture and colour. To achieve really successful cooking the fish should be of good quality and fresh. Choose whole, fillets, steaks or cutlets which are of even colour, firm to touch and do not have a strong odour. Unless you are used to preparing fish ask the fishmonger to clean and gut it for you. He will be able to advise you on the size and the weight that will be lost during cleaning. Store fish carefully, always wash it after purchase and store in a cool place, preferably the refrigerator. Fillets will only require rinsing and dabbing dry but whole fish may need to be scaled as well as cleaned and possibly skinned.

Whole cleaned fish can be cooked with the head on or removed. If you are at all squeamish it would be advisable to cook it without the head as the eyes have a tendency to pop out during cooking! The skin should be slashed two or three times on each side to allow the steam, which builds up inside the fish as it cooks, to escape. It is possible to cook very small fish for a few minutes without the risk of part of the fish overcooking, but medium or large whole fish will need to have delicate areas, such as the tail, shielded. By wrapping tiny pieces of smooth foil, shiny side inside, round the delicate areas of the fish the microwaves will be deflected and those areas will be cooked more by conduction than by microwaves, which will result in fairly even cooking. If the fish is large it may be necessary to remove the foil three-quarters of the way through cooking. Always lay the fish flat, in a single layer, and turn once during cooking. If two or more fish are to be cooked at one time they should be rearranged.

Fish fillets require slightly more attention to prevent uneven cooking. The thin tail ends must be shielded. This can be done in a number of ways: foil may be used in the same way as for cooking whole fish:

The tail ends may be tucked under the fish:

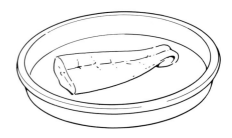

When several fillets are cooked at one time, the tails may be arranged so that they slightly overlap in the centre of the dish.

These guidelines should be followed when cooking fish:

Use only good quality fresh fish.

Whole fish should be slashed three times on each side, arrange fillets and cutlets with the thinnest part towards the centre of the dish.

Turn any cutlet or steak more than 1 inch (2.5cm) thick once during cooking.

When more than one fish or fillet is cooked at one time rearrange during cooking, for example turn rolled fillets 180 degrees. Arrange whole fish, cutlets, steaks or fillets in a single layer.

Add salt after cooking.

Cover with a lid or pierced clingfilm which doesn't have direct contact with the fish. Alternatively, if a crisp finish is required cover with a piece of greased greaseproof or non-stick paper.

Mussels and prawns may be cooked while live but all other live shellfish should not be cooked in a microwave oven.

Pierce or snip the corner of the bag before cooking boil-in-the-bag fish and remove any metallic labels.

Never overcook fish, always remove from the oven when slightly firm. Cooking should be completed during the standing time — if necessary it can always be returned to the oven.

Poached Salmon

Serves 2
190 Calories per serving

The following recipe is a basic method which can be adapted for cooking more or less any fish, just adjust the cooking times to suit the particular fish you are cooking.

---

2 × 5½oz (165g) salmon steaks

lemon juice

2 slices of lemon

1   Lay the salmon steaks in a shallow dish with the thinner part towards the centre, squeeze a little lemon juice over and lay a slice of lemon on top.

2   Cover and cook on HIGH for about 3 minutes 15 seconds, turn the steaks over halfway through the cooking time.

3   Leave to stand for 2 minutes and then serve, or leave covered and allow to cool then serve with a little lemon mayonnaise, but remember to add the additional Selections and calories.

Selections per serving:
4½ Protein

Cooking Guidelines for Fish

The following chart should be used as a guide. A little lemon juice may be squeezed over the fish but additional liquid will lengthen the cooking time. Leave the fish to stand 1½-2½ minutes after cooking.

Fish & Weight	No. Of Servings	Protein selection per serving	Calories per Serving	Setting	Time	Additional instructions
whole fish:						
1×6½oz (195g) dab	1	3	175	HIGH	2-2½ mins	Slash skin, shield head and tail, cover.
1×6oz (180g) mackerel	1	4	140	HIGH	3-3¼ mins	Slit skin, shield heads and tails, turn halfway through the cooking time, cover.
2×5oz (150g) red mullet	2	3½	160 each	HIGH	2-2½ mins	
2×5oz (150g) trout	2	3½	135 each	HIGH	3-3½ mins	
4oz (120g) sardines (3 whole fish)	1	3	150	HIGH	1-1½ mins	Slit skins, lay with tails overlapping, head shielded, cover.
fish steaks:						
1×5oz (150g) cod or hake	1	3½	115	HIGH	2-2½ mins	Turn halfway through the cooking time, cover.
2×5oz (150g) salmon	2	4	275	HIGH	3-3½ mins	Lay with thinner ends in centre of dish, turn halfway through the cooking time, cover.
1×4oz (120g) dense fish steak, eg swordfish	1	3	145	HIGH	1½-2 mins	Turn halfway through the cooking time, cover.
2×4oz (120g) dense fish steaks, eg tuna	2	3	195 each	HIGH	3-3½ mins	
fish fillets:						
1×8oz (240g) fillet cod, haddock (including smoked varieties)	2	3	180	HIGH	2-2½ mins	Cover.
2×4oz (120g) plaice fillets	2	3	110 each	HIGH	1¼-1½ mins	Lay with tails overlapping, cover.
4×4oz (120g) sole fillets	4	3	95 each	HIGH	1½-2 mins	
8oz (240g) plaice fillets	2	3	220	HIGH	3 mins	Add 4 tablespoons stock or milk (add additional calories), cover.

Fish Curry

Serves 4
200 Calories per serving

Use any variety of curry powder, hot Madras for a fiery taste or korma for a mild spicy flavour.

1 onion

6oz (180g) potatoes

6oz (180g) cauliflower florets

2oz (60g) okra

2 teaspoons oil

1½ tablespoons curry powder

½ tablespoon flour

8fl oz (240ml) stock or water

1lb 2oz (540g) skinned firm-fleshed white fish fillets e.g. monkfish, cod

1 medium banana

2oz (60g) frozen peas

lemon juice

Selections per serving:
  ½ Bread
  ½ Fat
  ½ Fruit
  3½ Protein
  1 Vegetable
  15 Optional Calories

1 Finely chop the onion. Cut the potato into 1-1½ inch (2.5-4cm) cubes.

2 Divide the cauliflower into small florets and cut the okra in half.

3 Place the oil, curry powder and onion in a container, cover and cook on HIGH for 1 minute 30 seconds.

4 Stir the flour into the onion and mix well then add the potatoes, cauliflower, okra and stock or water. Cover and cook on HIGH for 10 minutes.

5 Cut the fish into 2 inch (5cm) chunks.

6 Slice the banana.

7 Stir the fish, banana and frozen peas into the vegetable mixture, cover and cook on HIGH for 5 minutes.

8 Leave to stand 5 minutes then adjust the seasoning adding a little lemon juice if desired.

Kipper Pie

Serves 1
470 Calories per serving

By using a microwave it's possible to make and bake a pie for one in a very short time.

1 × 6oz (180g) potato

3½oz (105g) kipper fillet

1 tablespoon cornflour

¼ pint (150ml) skimmed milk

1 tablespoon finely chopped spring onion

1½oz (45g) cooked diced mixed vegetables

½ teaspoon lemon juice

salt and pepper

Selections per serving:
   2 Bread
   ½ Milk
   2½ Protein
   ½ Vegetable
   30 Optional Calories

1 Wash the potato, then prick several times using a fork and place in the oven on a double thickness of kitchen paper. Cook on HIGH for 3 minutes 30 seconds – 4 minutes or until cooked. Remove from the oven and leave to stand.

2 Lay the kipper fillet on a lipped plate, cover and cook on HIGH for 1 minute.

3 Place the cornflour in a jug or bowl. Reserve two tablespoons milk then gradually blend the remainder together with the cornflour. Cook, uncovered, on HIGH for 2 minutes, stirring twice during the cooking time.

4 Flake the kipper fillet, discard the skin and any remaining bones, add to the sauce together with the spring onion and mixed vegetables. Cook, uncovered on HIGH for 1 minute 30 seconds, stirring halfway through the cooking time until thick and boiling. Add the lemon juice.

5 Cut the potato in half, scoop out the inside and place in a bowl. Mash the potato with the reserved milk, season with salt and pepper.

6 Spoon the kipper and vegetable sauce into a small dish, spoon the mashed potato on top then return to the oven and cook on HIGH for 40 seconds. Leave to stand for 2 minutes.

Leek and Dab Dinner

Serves 1
300 Calories per serving

Dab is a small flat fish which should be eaten as fresh as possible. It may be cooked whole or with its head removed.

1 large leek

2 teaspoons margarine

grated zest and juice of ½ lemon

2 teaspoons chopped parsley

1 × 6½oz (195g) dab

Selections per serving:
2 Fat
3 Protein
1½ Vegetable

1   Finely slice the leek, place in a bowl with 1 teaspoon margarine. Cover and cook on HIGH for 1 minute 30 seconds or until the leek is tender.

2   Stir the lemon zest together with the slices of leek and parsley then arrange on an oval or rectangular dish large enough to hold the dab.

3   Make three slashes each side of the dab, sufficient to cut through the skin but not through the flesh.

4   Lay the dab on the leeks, pour over the lemon juice and dot with the remaining margarine. Cover and cook on HIGH for 2 minutes. Leave to stand for 2 minutes.

Hake with Herb Stuffing

Serves 2
225 Calories per serving

Cod or conger eel steaks could be used in place of hake.

2 × 5½oz (165g) hake steaks

1 tablespoon finely chopped fennel (the bulb, not feathery leaves)

2½ teaspoons magarine

1½oz (45g) breadcrumbs

¼ teaspoon tarragon

½ teaspoon parsley

finely grated zest of ¼ lemon

2 tablespoons skimmed milk

salt and pepper

Selections per serving:
  ¾ Bread
  1¼ Fat
  3½ Protein
  5 Optional Calories

1   Using a sharp knife remove the central bone from each fish steak. The skin will hold the flesh in one piece.

2   Place the fennel and 1 teaspoon margarine in a container, cover and cook on HIGH for 1 minute 15 seconds.

3   Mix the breadcrumbs together with the fennel, herbs and lemon zest.

4   Mix the milk into the breadcrumb mixture and stir well to bind. Season with a little salt and pepper.

5   Spoon the stuffing into the cavity left when the bones were removed from the fish steaks. Fold the skin round the stuffing and secure in place with wooden cocktail sticks.

6   Transfer the fish to a container, dot with the remaining margarine, cover and cook on HIGH for 3 minutes, rearranging halfway through the cooking time.

7   Leave the fish to stand 3 minutes, remove the cocktail sticks and serve.

Fish and Asparagus Flan

Serves 8
180 Calories per serving

The flan should be removed from the oven when it is not quite cooked in the centre but by the end of the standing time it should be completely set. If necessary return to the oven for a short time to complete the cooking.

1 × 8 inch (20cm) baked flan case (See page 219)

6oz (180g) smoked haddock fillet

6 tablespoons skimmed milk

4oz (120g) drained canned or cooked fresh or frozen asparagus

2 eggs

Selections per serving:
  ½ Bread
  1½ Fat
  ¾ Protein
  ¼ Vegetable
  55 Optional Calories

1   Place the flan case on a serving plate.

2   Lay the haddock on a lipped plate, add 4 tablespoons milk, cover and cook on HIGH for 2 minutes 30 seconds.

3   Cut the asparagus into 1-1½ inch (2.5-4cm) lengths.

4   Flake the fish into large flakes, discard the skin and any remaining bones, reserve the cooking liquid.

5   Spread the flakes of haddock and the asparagus evenly in the flan case.

6   Lightly beat the milk together with the eggs, liquid from cooking the fish and the remaining milk.

7   Spoon the egg mixture into the flan case and cook, uncovered, on MEDIUM for 6 minutes then LOW for 8 minutes until slightly wobbly in the centre. Leave to stand for 5 minutes.

Red Mullet in Vegetable Sauce

Serves 2
285 Calories per serving

Ask the fishmonger to clean the fish for you. I cook the fish with the heads on but if you prefer they may be removed and the cooking time reduced. The fish should weigh approximately 4oz (120g) cleaned and gutted.

2 × 5oz (150g) red mullet

1 onion

3oz (90g) frozen mixed peppers

4fl oz (120ml) tomato and mixed vegetable juice

3oz (90g) drained canned sweetcorn

1½ teaspoons chopped coriander

Selections per serving:
½ Bread
¼ Fruit
3 Protein
1 Vegetable

1 Clean the red mullet but leave the heads on. Make two or three slashes through each side of the fish.

2 Finely chop the onion, place in a bowl, cover and cook on HIGH for 2 minutes.

3 Add the peppers, cover and cook on HIGH for 2 minutes 30 seconds – do not add any water.

4 Stir the tomato and vegetable juice, sweetcorn and coriander into the pepper mixture and cook, uncovered, for 1 minute.

5 Spoon the vegetable mixture into a dish large enough to hold the fish in a single layer.

6 Lay the red mullet head to tail on top of the vegetable mixture, cover and cook on HIGH for 2 minutes. Remove from the oven and rearrange the fish so the side nearest the centre of the dish is turned towards the outer edge. Cover and cook on HIGH for a further 2 minutes. Leave to stand for 3 minutes.

Sardine Pâté

Serves 2
190 Calories per serving

This recipe is a cross between a dip and a pâté. Serve it with a salad or crudités and really fresh bread.

3 small sardines – total weight 4oz (120g)

2oz (60g) curd cheese

½ teaspoon lemon juice or vinegar

1 teaspoon tomato purée

1 teaspoon mayonnaise

10 capers

1 lemon

Selections per serving:
  ½ Fat
  2 Protein
  5 Optional Calories

1 Arrange the sardines in a circle with the tails slightly overlapping. Place a very small piece of foil over the tails and cover with pierced clingfilm – the film should not be in contact with the fish.

2 Cook the sardines on HIGH for 1 minute then leave to cool.

3 Open the sardines and gently lift the central bone and as many of the smaller bones as possible. Discard the bones and skin and place the flesh in a bowl.

4 Mash the sardines and remove as many small bones as possible. Add the curd cheese, lemon juice, tomato purée and mayonnaise. Mash well.

5 Finely chop the capers and stir into the sardine mixture. Cut the lemon in half lengthways and, using a grapefruit knife, scoop out the centre including the membranes. Keep the juice and membranes, they can be pushed through a nylon sieve and used as lemon juice in other recipes.

6 Spoon the Sardine Pâté into the lemon halves and roughen the surface with a fork. Refrigerate until the pâté is to be served.

Smoked Trout and Courgette Mousse

Serves 6
150 Calories per serving

Only about half the weight of smoked trout is suitable for use, there should be a total of 6-7oz (180-210g) fish from two trout.

½ pint (300ml) skimmed milk

few slices of onion

finely grated zest of ½ lemon

14oz (420g) young courgettes

salt

2 tablespoons cornflour

2 large eggs (size 1), separated

2 × 5oz (150g) smoked trout, skinned and flaked

6 tablespoons soured cream

2 tablespoons gelatine

pinch of cream of tartar

1 Pour the milk into a jug or bowl, add the onion and lemon zest and heat on HIGH for 2 minutes, leave to infuse for 20-30 minutes, or longer if possible.

2 Using a potato peeler remove thin slices along the length of two courgettes to give about twelve slices with a green border of courgette skin either side.

3 Lay the slices of courgette in a sieve, sprinkle with salt and leave for 15-20 minutes to draw out some of their liquid. Rinse well then lay flat in a container, cover and cook on HIGH for 2 minutes.

4 Roughly chop the remaining courgette, cover and cook on HIGH for 4 minutes.

5 Place the cornflour in a jug, strain the milk then gradually blend into the cornflour. Cook, uncovered, on HIGH for about 4 minutes 30 seconds stirring frequently. Allow to cool for 3 minutes then stir well. Beat the egg yolks and then stir into the sauce. Cook on LOW for about 1 minute or until the egg yolks slightly thicken the sauce.

6 Pour the sauce into a liquidiser. Add the trout, chopped courgettes and soured cream. Process to a smooth purée.

7   Place 3 tablespoons water and the gelatine in a small bowl or cup. Heat on HIGH for 40 seconds, stir well until the gelatine has dissolved. Reserve 1 teaspoon of the dissolved gelatine, add the remainder to the purée and process once again. Pour the purée into a bowl and chill until thick and beginning to set.

8   Add 2 tablespoons water to the reserved gelatine, brush round the inside of a 2½ pint (1.5 litre) ring mould. Drain the slices of courgette well, pat thoroughly with kitchen paper – they must be dry – then arrange in the mould.

9   Whisk the egg whites and cream of tartar until peaking, fold into the setting trout mixture, spoon into the mould and leave until completely set.

Selections per serving:
1½ Protein
75 Optional Calories

10 Just before serving dip the mould briefly in hot water then invert onto a serving plate.

Soft Roe Quickie

Serves 1
225 Calories per serving

Soft roes cook extremely quickly in the microwave but they must be covered as they frequently splatter during cooking.

2 teaspoons margarine

4 teaspoons finely chopped spring onion

3oz (90g) soft herring roes

lemon juice

salt and pepper

1oz (30g) slice of toast

1   Place 1 teaspoon margarine and the spring onion in a bowl and microwave on HIGH for 40 seconds.

2   Remove any veins on the roes and place in the bowl with the spring onion.

3   Cover the bowl and microwave on HIGH for 45 seconds. Leave to stand for 1 minute then transfer to a serving plate.

4   Sprinkle the roes liberally with lemon juice and sprinkle with salt and pepper.

5   Spread the toast with the remaining margarine and serve with the hot roes.

Selections per serving:
1 Bread
2 Fat
2 Protein

Stuffed Trout

Serves 2
195 Calories per serving

Arrange the trout in a shallow dish with the head of one fish beside the tail of the other. Use very small pieces of foil to shield the delicate areas of the fish, it must never come in contact with the oven.

---

2 × 5oz (150g) trout, cleaned

2½oz (75g) fennel

1 teaspoon margarine

1 tablespoon finely chopped chives

1 tablespoon finely chopped parsley

1oz (30g) fresh breadcrumbs

1 teaspoon lemon juice

Selections per serving:
  ½ Bread
  ½ Fat
  3½ Protein
  ½ Vegetable

1 Make five incisions across each side of the trout, they should just slit the skin not cut into the flesh.

2 Chop the fennel as finely as possible.

3 Place the margarine and fennel in a bowl or small container, cover and cook on HIGH for 2 minutes

4 Stir the herbs, breadcrumbs and lemon juice together with the fennel. Mix well.

5 Spoon the stuffing into the trout then lay in an oblong or oval shallow dish. Lay four small pieces of foil, shiny side against the fish, over the trout tails and heads – make sure the foil is very smooth.

6 Cover the dish and cook on HIGH for 3 mintues 30 seconds – 4 minutes, rearrange halfway through the cooking time. Leave to stand for 3 minutes.

Seaman's Terrine

Serves 8
120 Calories per serving

Use a sharp knife to cut the terrine in slices then serve with a selection of vegetables or a mixed salad.

1½lb (720g) skinned cod fillet

1 large egg

3oz (90g) fresh white breadcrumbs

finely grated zest of 1 lemon

3-4 tablespoons chopped chives

salt and pepper

6oz (180g) skinned trout fillet

Selections per serving:
  ¼ Bread
  3 Protein
  10 Optional Calories

1   Line the base of a loaf dish approximately 8½ × 4½ inches (21.5 × 11.5cm) with non-stick baking parchment.

2   Place the cod, egg and breadcrumbs in a food processor and process to a purée. Transfer the cod purée to a bowl and stir in the lemon zest and chives. Season well with salt and pepper.

3   Cut the trout into thin lengths so they will fit into the loaf dish.

4   Lay three of four strips of trout along the base of the loaf dish. Spoon half the cod mixture on top and press down firmly. Arrange a few more strips of trout in the dish and cover with the remaining cod mixture and then arrange the remaining trout on top. Press the mixture firmly and evenly with the back of a spoon.

5   Cover the dish with a piece of pierced clingfilm, making sure it is not in contact with the fish, and cook on HIGH for 11 minutes. Leave to stand for 7-8 minutes then turn out onto a serving plate.

Friday's Fish

Serves 4
130 Calories per serving

The variety of vegetables can be altered according to what you have to hand.
Refer to the vegetable cooking chart on pages 145-146 to decide when they
should be added to the recipe.

1 large onion

1 clove garlic

2oz (60g) fennel

3 sticks celery

4oz (120g) carrot

3oz (90g) baby corn on the cob

¼ pint (150ml) stock

2 tablespoons chopped parsley

8fl oz (240ml) tomato and vegetable juice

3oz (90g) broccoli florets

1lb (480g) mixture of boneless firm white fish e.g. monkfish, huss

Selections per serving:
  ¼ Bread
  ¼ Fruit
  3½ Protein
  1½ Vegetable

1   Chop the onion, garlic and fennel.

2   Slice the celery and carrot. Cut the baby corn on the cob in half.

3   Place the onion, garlic, fennel, celery, carrot and corn in a container, add 6 tablespoons stock, cover and cook on HIGH for 12 minutes.

4   Stir the remaining stock, parsley and the tomato and vegetable juice into the hot vegetables.

5   Thinly slice the broccoli stalks and divide the head of each floret into small pieces.

6   Cut the fish into 1 inch (2.5cm) chunks.

7   Stir the broccoli and fish into the vegetables.

8   Cover the dish and cook on HIGH for 6 minutes, stirring halfway through the cooking time.

9   Leave to stand for 4 minutes.

Tuna Kebabs

Serves 4
100 Calories per serving

Many fishmongers and supermarkets now sell fresh tuna but if you are unable to buy it substitute monkfish and reduce the cooking time by about 30 seconds.

juice of ½ lemon

1 teaspoon oil

½ teaspoon chilli powder

10oz (300g) tuna

few onion rings

6oz (180g) courgettes

4 lemon wedges

Selections per serving:
  ¼ Fat
  2 Protein
  ½ Vegetable

1 Using a fork whisk the lemon juice together with the oil and chilli powder.

2 Cut the tuna into ¾ inch (2cm) squares.

3 Lay the tuna in a non-metallic dish, pour over the lemon juice mixture, add the onion rings and cover. Leave to marinate for 2-3 hours.

4 Cut the courgettes into ¾ inch (2cm) thick slices.

5 Thread the tuna and courgette slices onto four wooden skewers. Lay the skewers on a plate and spoon the marinade over them.

6 Cover the dish and cook on HIGH for 4 – 4 minutes 30 seconds, rearrange halfway through the cooking time. Leave to stand for 2 minutes then serve with the cooking juices spooned over the top and garnish with lemon wedges.

Rolled Plaice Fillets

Serves 4
170 Calories per serving

Serve this recipe with a selection of colourful vegetables.

4 × 3½oz (105g) skinned plaice fillets

3oz (90g) breadcrumbs

1 tablespoon chopped parsley

1 tablespoon chopped chives

½ teaspoon oregano

finely grated zest of 1 lemon

1 tablespoon lemon juice

1 egg, beaten

Selections per serving:
  ¾ Bread
  3 Protein

1 Lay the plaice fillets with the sides which had been attached to the skin facing upwards.

2 Mix the breadcrumbs together with herbs and lemon zest. Add the lemon juice and egg and mix well.

3 Spread the stuffing over each fillet, do not spread it completely across the fish – leave a thin space along the length of the fillets.

4 Roll the fillets loosely from the tail end towards the head. Secure the rolls with wooden cocktail sticks.

5 Transfer the Rolled Plaice Fillets to a container and arrange in a circular pattern.

6 Cover the dish and cook on HIGH for 2 minutes then rearrange the fish and cook on HIGH for 1 minute 30 seconds. Leave to stand for 4 minutes.

Herring Rolls

Serves 4
300 Calories per serving

This recipe is an adaptation of the traditional Soused Herrings but it isn't as acidic because the vinegar has been replaced with fruit juice. Orange and lemon juices give a tangy flavour which complements the richness of the fish.

4 × 4oz (120g) herring fillets

1 medium orange

1 lemon

1 small onion

Selections per serving:
 ¼ Fruit
 3 Protein
 ¼ Vegetable

1   Trim the fins off the fishes.

2   Roll each fillet, skin-side outside, from the tail to the head then secure in place with a wooden cocktail stick.

3   Remove the orange and lemon zests from the fruits with a zester or pare thinly with a potato peeler and cut into very thin fine strips.

4   Squeeze the juice from the fruits. Pour the juice into a container, add the zest and lay the fish in a circle. Thinly slice the onion and add to the container.

5   Cover the container and cook on HIGH for 3 minutes 30 seconds, rearrange the fish once during cooking. Leave until cold.

Herring Rolls and Seafood Savoury (see page 72)

Seafood Savoury

Serves 2
150 Calories per serving

This recipe includes scampi tails and prawns, but if you prefer, a variety of shellfish can be used.

1 tablespoon cornflour

¼ pint (150ml) skimmed milk

1 tablespoon tomato purée

1 tablespoon chopped chives

4 teaspoons chopped parsley

2½oz (75g) scampi tails

2½oz (75g) peeled prawns

salt and pepper

2 tablespoons sherry

1 Blend the cornflour together with the milk, stir in the tomato purée and chives. Reserve 1 teaspoon parsley, stir the remainder into the sauce mixture.

2 Place the sauce in the oven and cook, uncovered, for 1 minute 30 seconds.

3 Stir well then continue cooking for about 2 minutes, stirring every 30 seconds until the sauce thickens and boils.

4 Stir the scampi tails and prawns into the sauce and cook, uncovered on HIGH for 1 minute 20 seconds.

5 Remove from the oven, leave to stand 2 minutes then season with salt and pepper and stir in the sherry.

6 Spoon the Seafood Savoury into a serving dish and sprinkle with the remaining parsley.

Selections per serving:
  ¼ Milk
  2 Protein
  35 Optional Calories

Fish Pie

Serves 4
265 Calories per serving

Although the cheese will melt on top of the pie it won't brown. If you prefer a golden brown potato topping place under a hot grill for 1-2 minutes.

8oz (240g) cod or haddock fillet

1 onion, finely chopped

2oz (60g) mushrooms, roughly chopped

3oz (90g) frozen mixed vegetables

1lb (480g) potatoes, cut into 1½ inch (4cm) cubes

12fl oz (360ml) skimmed milk

1oz (30g) cornflour

3oz (90g) peeled prawns

2oz (60g) cooked mussels – out of shell

1½ tablespoons chopped parsley

salt and pepper

1 tomato, sliced

½oz (15g) cheese, finely grated

Selections per serving:
  1½ Bread
  ¼ Milk
  3 Protein
  1 Vegetable
  10 Optional Calories

1. Lay the cod or haddock on a lipped plate, cover with pierced clingfilm – it should not be in direct contact with the fish – and cook on HIGH for 1 minute 30 seconds.

2. Place the onion in a suitable container. Drain the liquid from the cod, add the onion, cover and cook on HIGH for 2 minutes 30 seconds.

3. Stir the mushrooms and frozen mixed vegetables into the onion then cover and cook on HIGH for 3 minutes.

4. Place the potato cubes in a container, add 5 tablespoons water and cook on HIGH for 8 minutes.

5. Reserve 4 tablespoons milk, blend the remainder with the cornflour, then cook on HIGH for 5 minutes, stirring frequently. Flake the cod then stir it, together with the prawns, mussels, onion mixture and parsley into the sauce. Cook on HIGH for 2 minutes 30 seconds, stirring every minute. Season with salt and pepper.

6. Drain the potatoes and mash with the reserved milk.

7. Spoon the fish sauce into a serving dish, top with the mashed potato and roughen the surface with a fork. Cook on HIGH for 3 minutes, arrange the tomato slices on top and sprinkle with cheese. Cook for a further 30 seconds. Leave to stand for 3-4 minutes.

Sole and Salmon Circles

Serves 4
90 Calories per serving

If you wish, the sole and salmon may be left to cool then sliced and served cold on a bed of lettuce and accompanied by mayonnaise – remember to add 1 Fat Selection or 40 Calories for every teaspoon of mayonnaise.

4 × 3oz (90g) skinned sole fillets

1½oz (45g) smoked salmon

1 tablespoon finely chopped chervil

juice of ½ lemon

4 lemon wedges

few sprigs of chervil

1 Lay the sole fillets on a flat surface with the sides which had been attached to the skin facing upwards.

2 Cut the slices of smoked salmon into four strips and lay a strip along each sole fillet.

3 Sprinkle the chervil evenly over the salmon then roll up Swiss roll fashion.

4 Secure the fish rolls with one or two wooden cocktail sticks.

5 Arrange the fish in a circular pattern round a lipped plate or dish. Pour the lemon juice over the rolls, cover and cook on HIGH for 1 minute 30 seconds then rearrange the rolls, turning them 180 degrees and cook on HIGH for 1 minute 30 seconds. Leave to stand for 2 minutes then transfer to a chopping board and cut each roll into four or five slices. Arrange the slices on serving plates and garnish each plate with a lemon wedge and sprig of chervil.

Selections per serving:
  2¾ Protein

Sole and Salmon Circles and Pineberry Mousse (see page 191)

Fish with Prawn Sauce

Serves 2
165 Calories per serving

This recipe can be prepared with ingredients which are in most kitchens or stored in the freezer. One of the advantages of the microwave oven is the speed it can defrost food. Remember the temperature of food drastically affects cooking times. If your freezer is kept at 'Fast Freeze' the fish will require a longer cooking time. If the sauce is prepared before assembling the dish the prawns should not be added; reheat the sauce, add the prawns then continue.

1½oz (45g) frozen prawns

6fl oz (180ml) skimmed milk

1½ tablespoons cornflour

salt and pepper

6oz (180g) frozen mixed vegetables

2 × 3oz (90g) frozen boneless cod, plaice or haddock steaks

Selections per serving:
¼ Milk
3¼ Protein
¼ Vegetable
30 Optional Calories

1   Spread the prawns evenly over a plate and cook on LOW for 1 minute – remove from the oven and set aside to complete thawing.

2   Blend the milk together with the cornflour, place in the oven and cook on HIGH for 1 minute, stir well and cook for a further 1 minute 30 seconds. Stir in the prawns and season to taste with salt and pepper.

3   Place the mixed vegetables in two suitable containers. Spread them evenly so they just cover the base of each dish. Cover and cook on HIGH for 2 minutes 30 seconds.

4   Remove the dishes from the oven and stir the vegetables, they should be hot but not completely cooked. Pour off any liquid from the vegetables.

5   Lay the frozen fish steaks on top of the vegetables and pour the prawn sauce over. Cover the dish and cook on HIGH for 8 minutes 30 seconds. Leave covered for 2-3 minutes.

Sole Véronique

Serves 4
185 Calories per serving

It may seem unnecessary to skin all the grapes but it is well worth the trouble as the texture of grapes without their skins is beautifully smooth.

---

4 tablespoons white wine

3oz (90g) seedless white grapes

4 teaspoons cornflour

6 tablespoons skimmed milk

4 tablespoons single cream

4 × 4oz (120g) skinned sole or plaice fillets

2 teaspoons grated Parmesan cheese

1   Place the wine and grapes in a small bowl or cup so the wine just covers the grapes. Place uncovered in the microwave and cook on HIGH for 1 minute.

2   Remove the grapes from the wine with a slotted spoon. Peel the skins off the grapes, then cut them in half and put to one side.

3   Blend the cornflour to a paste with the milk, then stir in the cream and warm wine.

4   Lay the fish fillets on a large plate with the tail ends of the fillets slightly overlapping in the centre. Cover the plate and cook on HIGH for 1 minute 30 seconds.

5   Place the cornflour mixture in the oven and cook on HIGH for 3 minutes, stirring every 50-60 seconds. Add the grapes and any juices which have run from the fish. Stir well.

6   Arrange the fish on a serving plate, spoon the sauce over the top and sprinkle with the Parmesan cheese. Return to the oven for 30-40 seconds. Brown under a preheated grill if desired.

Selections per serving:
   ¼ Fruit
   3 Protein
   85 Optional Calories

Prawns in Saffron Sauce

Serves 2
145 Calories per serving

Use good quality saffron for this recipe. Saffron that is poor quality or which has been stored for a long time gives very little flavour. Always keep the grains in a dark airtight container.

6fl oz (180ml) skimmed milk

few grains saffron

1½ teaspoons finely chopped chervil

1 teaspoon finely chopped chives

4 teaspoons cornflour

4oz (120g) peeled prawns

2 tablespoons single cream

salt and pepper

Selections per serving:
  ¼ Milk
  2 Protein
  75 Optional Calories

1 Pour 4 tablespoons milk into a cup or small basin, add two or three grains saffron, the chervil and chives.

2 Cook on HIGH for 40 seconds until the milk is steaming, not boiling. Leave the milk to infuse for several hours, if possible overnight.

3 Blend the cornflour together with the infused milk then gradually add the remaining milk.

4 Cook the Saffron Sauce on HIGH for 1 minute 30 seconds, stir halfway through the cooking time.

5 Stir the prawns and cream into the sauce and cook for 50-60 seconds, stir well then season to taste with salt and pepper.

Squid in Fresh Tomato Sauce

Serves 2
140 Calories per serving

Squid are often sold with their heads already removed. If you buy them whole allow about an extra ounce (30g) in weight then remove the heads and tentacles. The tentacles may be chopped and added to the sauce.

1 large clove garlic

1 leek

½ red pepper

10oz (300g) tomatoes

½ teaspoon basil

½ teaspoon marjoram

4 × 2oz (60g) squid, heads removed

Selections per serving:
3 Protein
2½ Vegetable

1   Finely chop the garlic, leek and red pepper.

2   Chop the tomatoes – there is no need to skin them first.

3   Place the garlic, leek, red pepper and tomatoes in a container, stir in the herbs and cook on HIGH for 7 minutes.

4   Clean the squid. Pull out the plastic-looking backbone from the inside of each squid and wash the fish well. Remove any soft white substance from the inside and peel off the purple-coloured skin from the body. Cut the body of the squid into thin rings.

5   Stir the squid rings into the hot cooked vegetables, cover and cook on HIGH for 2 minutes. Leave to stand for 2 minutes.

Creamy Scallops

Serves 4
90 Calories per serving

Make this recipe into a substantial snack by piping a ring of hot mashed potato around the edge of the serving dishes. Add the additional Selections and calories as necessary.

6oz (180g) scallops

2 spring onions

½ clove garlic

1 teaspoon margarine

½ tablespoon cornflour

4 tablespoons white wine

4 tablespoons single cream

2 teaspoons finely chopped parsley

½-1 teaspoon lemon juice

salt and pepper

4 lemon wedges

Selections per serving:
  ¼ Fat
  1¼ Protein
  70 Optional Calories

1 Remove and reserve the corals from the scallops. Thickly slice the white part of each scallop.

2 Thinly slice the spring onions and crush the garlic.

3 Place the spring onions, garlic and margarine in a bowl, cover and cook on HIGH for 1 minute.

4 Sprinkle the cornflour into the bowl, stir well then add the wine, cream and 1 teaspoon parsley. Cover and cook on HIGH for 1 minute, stirring once during cooking.

5 Stir the scallops into the cream and wine sauce and cook on HIGH for 2 minutes 30 seconds, stirring halfway through the cooking time. Leave to stand for 2 minutes, season to taste with lemon juice, salt and pepper.

6 Spoon the mixture into four scallop dishes or ramekins, sprinkle with the remaining parsley and garnish with lemon wedges.

Dairy

Milk, cheese and eggs are all dairy products which are high in protein and require careful cooking to obtain an even texture. The structure of proteins change during cooking: milk forms a skin, cheese toughens and becomes stringy, eggs set and eventually curdle.

MILK

When milk is heated the proteins set and form a skin. The skin acts in the same way as a lid and if heating continues the milk pushes up, lifts the skin and overflows. Milk should always be heated in a large bowl or jug with the container never more than two-thirds full. It can be heated in a microwave without the risk of sticking and burning which often occurs in a saucepan, especially when cooking a small quantity. Cornflour-based sauces, which are particularly desirable for the weight conscious, can be made in just a few minutes.

Basic Savoury Sauces

As a microwave is particularly useful for making small quantities of sauces I am including a Basic Bechamel Sauce which uses only ¼ pint (150ml) skimmed milk and is sufficient for two servings. This sauce can be used as a guide for making the same quantity of numerous sauces, sweet and savoury. For example if you wish to make ¼ pint (150ml) custard omit the onion, cloves, salt and pepper and use 1 tablespoon custard powder in place of the cornflour. Omit the infusing time but follow exactly the same method and blend all the ingredients together, adding sweetening as desired, then cook on high for 2 minutes 30 seconds, stirring every 20-30 seconds.

Basic Bechamel Sauce

Serves 2
50 Calories per serving

¼ pint (150ml) skimmed milk

¼-½ onion

4 whole cloves

1 tablespoon cornflour

salt and pepper

1 Place the milk, onion and cloves in a jug or bowl and microwave on HIGH for 1 minute 30 seconds. Set aside and leave for 15-20 minutes or until cool.

2 Strain the milk and gradually blend into the cornflour.

3 Place the sauce in the oven and cook on HIGH for 2 minutes 30 seconds, stirring after the first minute and then every 20-30 seconds, until it has boiled and thickened. Remove the sauce from the oven and season with salt and pepper.

Selections per serving:
¼ Milk
15 Optional Calories

The following recipes are for 'coating' consistency sauces; if a thinner sauce is required decrease the quantity of cornflour by one tablespoon and deduct 10 Calories per serving.

Coating White Sauce

Serves 4
50 Calories per serving

2 tablespoons cornflour

½ pint (300ml) skimmed milk

1 Spoon the cornflour into a jug, gradually blend in the milk.

2 Place the jug in the oven and cook, uncovered, on HIGH for 4 minutes 30 seconds, stirring after the first 1 minute 30 seconds then every 40 seconds. The sauce should be boiling and smooth.

3 Remove the sauce from the oven and season with salt and pepper if it is to be served as a savoury white sauce, or add the following ingredients to make sweet or savoury sauces.

Selections per serving:
¼ Milk
15 Optional Calories

VARIATIONS
Add the following to the hot sauce, stir well and if necessary return to the oven and re-heat on HIGH for a few seconds.

Savoury Sauces

Parsley or Chive Sauce
Add 2 tablespoons finely chopped herbs.
50 Calories per serving
Selections per serving:
¼ Milk
15 Optional Calories

Cheese Sauce
Add 3½oz (105g) grated cheese and ¼ teaspoon mustard.
150 Calories per serving
Selections per serving:
¼ Milk
¾ Protein
25 Optional Calories

Prawn Sauce
Add 4oz (120g) roughly chopped prawns and a squeeze of lemon juice.
80 Calories per serving.
Selections per serving:
¼ Milk
1 Protein
15 Optional Calories

Egg Sauce
Add 1 finely chopped hard-boiled egg.
70 Calories per serving
Selections per serving:
¼ Milk
¼ Protein
15 Optional Calories

Sweet Sauces

Sweet White Sauce
Add 1 tablespoon sugar and 2-3 drops vanilla essence.
65 Calories per serving
Selections per serving:
¼ Milk
30 Optional Calories

Chocolate Sauce
Add 1 tablespoon cocoa, 1½ tablespoons sugar and 2-3 drops vanilla essence to the cornflour, then blend in the milk.
75 Calories per serving
Selections per serving:
¼Milk
45 Optional Calories

Ginger Sauce
Add 1 tablespoon golden syrup, finely grated zest ½ lemon and ½ teaspoon ground ginger to the blended cornflour and milk. Add a little lemon juice to the cooked sauce.
65 Calories per serving
Selections per serving:
¼ Milk
30 Optional Calories

Custard Sauce

Serves 4
80 Calories per serving

**2 tablespoons custard powder or
1 × 1 pint (600ml) sachet**

1 pint (600ml) skimmed milk

1 tablespoon sugar

1 Spoon the custard powder into a large jug, gradually blend in the milk then stir in the sugar.

2 Place the jug in the oven and cook, uncovered, on HIGH for 6-7 minutes, stirring after the first 2 minutes and then every 40-50 seconds, until it has boiled and thickened.

Selections per serving:
½ Milk
30 Optional Calories

Stirred Egg Custard

Serves 4
75 Calories per serving

Do not overcook this custard, it will thicken slightly after cooking. It is important to whisk several times during the cooking time to prevent the egg setting round the edge of the bowl or jug.

½ pint (300ml) skimmed milk

2 eggs

1 tablespoon sugar

few drops of vanilla essence

1 Pour the milk into a basin or jug. Microwave, uncovered, on HIGH for 2 minutes until hot but not boiling.

2 Lightly whisk the eggs, add the milk then strain into the basin or jug.

3 Stir the sugar and vanilla essence into the custard and cook, uncovered, on HIGH for 1 minute.

4 Remove the custard from the oven and whisk well then return to the oven and cook, uncovered, on LOW for 4 minutes 30 seconds. Whisk or stir well several times during the cooking time. Remove from the oven when the custard thinly coats the back of a spoon.

Selections per serving:
¼ Milk
½ Protein
15 Optional Calories

CHEESE

Cheese cooked in the microwave oven requires the same treatment as conventional methods. It should never be overcooked. Cheese melts quickly when microwaved but it doesn't have the traditional golden brown appearance. To obtain this colour it is necessary to transfer the completed recipe to a conventional grill, but check the dish is suitable for use under direct heat – many microwave-safe dishes are not.

The following recipe for Welsh Rarebit is simple and allows for many variations. For example each serving may be topped with a poached egg to make Buck Rarebit, or a few slices of tomato or onion may be arranged on the toast before the cheese is poured over. The combinations are endless.

Welsh Rarebit

Serves 1 or 2
265 Calories per serving

---

1 × 1oz (30g) slice hot toast

1½oz (45g) cheese, grated

dash of Worcestershire sauce

¼ teaspoon mustard

1 tablespoon milk

1 Lay the toast on a microwave-safe plate.

2 Place all the remaining ingredients in a bowl and cook on MEDIUM for 20 seconds, stir well then spoon on top of the hot toast. Place the plate in the oven and cook on MEDIUM for 15 seconds until bubbling. If preferred the recipe may be completed under a conventional grill to give a golden appearance.

To serve 2:

2 × 1oz (30g) slices hot toast

3oz (90g) cheese, grated

dash of Worcestershire sauce

½ teaspoon mustard

2 tablespoons milk

1 Arrange the toast on two microwave-safe plates.

2 Place all the remaining ingredients in a bowl and cook on MEDIUM for 1 minute. Stir well then spoon onto the slices of toast and place in the oven and cook on MEDIUM for 30 seconds – if the plates won't fit side-by-side in the oven reheat each one separately for 15 seconds.

Selections per serving:
1 Bread
1½ Protein
5 Optional Calories

EGGS

The structure of egg proteins change during heating. They set and, if heating continues, eventually curdle. Eggs in shells are not suitable for microwave cooking as the build-up of pressure results in them exploding out of their shells. Contrary to popular belief it is possible to cook soft and hard-boiled eggs in a microwave oven. The eggs should be wrapped in foil, placed in a cup or bowl and completely covered with water. The cup or bowl should then be placed, uncovered, in the microwave and as the water boils the eggs will cook in exactly the same way as boiling in a saucepan. The eggs are cooked by the conduction of heat as the water boils, not by the microwaves which heat the water. As the cooking time is more or less the same as conventional cooking there is little point in carrying out such a procedure, particularly as it is unwise to become accustomed to using foil.

All food encased in a skin must be pierced before cooking. Egg yolks are surrounded by membranes which must always be punctured to prevent the yolk bursting out and exploding over the walls of the oven.

Eggs cook well in the microwave and it is possible to poach, bake, scramble and fry them very successfully. Usually a MEDIUM heat is desirable so the eggs cook gently and the cooking is then completed during the standing time. Whole eggs cooked in the microwave cook in the opposite way from conventional methods: the yolk, which contains a high proportion of fat, attracts the microwaves and cooks before the white. The conduction of heat from the yolk cooks the white.

Baked Eggs

Serves 1 or 2
90 Calories per serving

¼ teaspoon margarine

1 egg

1 Grease a ramekin with the margarine.

2 Break the egg into the greased ramekin then pierce the yolk with a cocktail stick.

3 Cover the ramekin tightly with clingfilm – it must not touch the egg – and cook on MEDIUM for 1 minute 30 seconds. Leave to stand for 1 minute then carefully remove the film.

To serve 2:

½ teaspoon margarine

2 eggs

1 Grease two ramekins with the margarine.

2 Break one egg into each ramekin then pierce the yolks with a cocktail stick.

3 Cover the ramekins tightly with clingfilm, making sure it does not touch the eggs, and arrange on opposite sides of the oven. Cook on MEDIUM for 2 minutes 10 seconds. Leave to stand for 1 minute then carefully remove the clingfilm.

Selections per serving:
¼ Fat
1 Protein

Poached Eggs

Serves 1 or 2
80 Calories per serving

---

1 egg

5 tablespoons boiling water

¼ teaspoon vinegar

1 Break the egg onto a saucer, pierce the yolk gently with a cocktail stick.

2 Pour the water into a small bowl, add the vinegar and cook on HIGH until boiling. Leave the bowl in the oven and slide in the egg, cover tightly with clingfilm. Cook on MEDIUM for 30 seconds. Leave 1 minute then remove the film and, using a slotted spoon, life the egg onto a plate.

To serve 2:

2 eggs

½ pint (300ml) boiling water

½ teaspoon vinegar

1 Break each egg onto a saucer and pierce the yolks with a cocktail stick.

2 Pour the boiling water into a shallow dish about 7-8 inches (17.5-20cm) long. Add the vinegar and cook on HIGH until boiling. Slide the eggs into the boiling water, cover tightly with clingfilm. Cook on MEDIUM for 1 minute 30 seconds. Leave 1 minute then remove the film and, using a slotted spoon, lift the eggs out of the water.

Selections per serving:
  1 Protein

Fried Eggs

Serves 1 or 2
100 Calories per serving

The microwave browning plate or griddle must be very hot so the egg is half cooked immediately it touches the surface.

½ teaspoon oil

1 egg

1 Heat the browning plate according to the manufacturer's instructions.

2 Spoon the oil onto the hot plate and using oven gloves tilt slightly so the oil spreads out. Break the egg onto the hot plate and pierce the yolk. If the plate has a cover place in position, if not I prefer to cook it uncovered rather than mess about trying to place an upturned bowl over a hot griddle. Cook on HIGH for 45 seconds.

To serve 2:

1 teaspoon oil

2 eggs

1 Break the eggs onto separate saucers, pierce the yolks with a cocktail stick. This is necessary to cook the eggs quickly; time is saved since the yolks are already pierced. Heat the browning plate according to the manufacturer's instructions.

2 Spoon the oil onto the hot plate and using oven gloves tilt the dish so the oil spreads. Quickly slide the eggs onto the hot plate, if it has a cover place in position, if not leave uncovered. Cook on HIGH for 1 minute 10 seconds.

Selections per serving:
  ½ Fat
  1 Protein

The microwave oven cooks scrambled eggs very well without the risk of the mixture sticking and burning. I have suggested 1 teaspoon margarine is added to every egg as this gives a creamy texture and prevents the mixture sticking to the edge of the bowl or jug. If you prefer the margarine may be omitted and the Fat Selection or 40 Calories deducted per serving.

Use a jug or a container with a narrow diameter, otherwise the egg will start to set round the edge of the dish. Cooking on a MEDIUM power reduces the risk of overcooking, but to obtain the creamy consistency the mixture must be removed from the oven frequently and whisked from the outer edge towards the centre. Do not replace the bowl in the oven with the whisk. Lay it on a plate ready for use. Remove the mixture from the oven while it is still a little liquid in the centre. Cooking must be completed during the standing time, if necessary it can always be returned to the oven for a few more seconds.

Chopped chives, grated cheese or diced ham may be added to the mixture before cooking but remember to calculate the additional Selections and calories.

Scrambled Eggs

Serves 1 or 2:
135 Calories per serving

1 teaspoon margarine

1 egg

2 tablespoons milk

salt and pepper

1   Whisk all the ingredients together in a bowl or jug.

2   Cook on MEDIUM for 40 seconds, remove from the oven and whisk well, cook for a further minute whisking every 20 seconds. Leave to stand for 1 minute.

To serve 2:

2 teaspoons margarine

2 eggs

4 tablespoons milk

salt and pepper

1   Whisk all the ingredients together in a bowl or jug.

2   Cook the mixture on MEDIUM for 1 minute 30 seconds, remove from the oven and whisk well, cook for a further minute whisking the mixture every 20 seconds. Leave to stand for 1 minute.

Selections per serving:
    1 Fat
    1 Protein
    10 Optional Calories

Omelettes may be cooked on round plates with a slight lip or on hot browning plates. This recipe gives the method for using a plate but if you prefer use a browning plate and follow the manufacturer's instructions. The omelette may be browned a little by placing it under a preheated very hot grill for a few seconds, but do not overcook or it will have a rubbery texture.

The recipe below may be used as a basic recipe for sweet or savoury variations. Add herbs before cooking but add cooked vegetables or meat just after the mixture has been stirred. If you wish to make a sweet jam omelette spread the jam on the omelette after the standing period. The jam may be warmed in the oven while the omelette is left to stand. Always remember to add the additional Selections or calories.

Omelette

Serves 1
215 Calories per serving

1½ teaspoons margarine

2 eggs

1 tablespoon water

salt and pepper

1 Place the margarine on a 7½-8 inch (17.5-20cm) lipped plate. Cook on HIGH for 40 seconds until melted.

2 Whisk the eggs together with water and a little salt and pepper.

3 Tilt the plate to coat with the melted margarine. Pour the eggs onto the plate and cook uncovered, on HIGH for 1 minute, draw the setting edge towards the centre and cook on HIGH for 1 minute 40 seconds or until just a little wobbly in the centre. Leave to stand for 50-60 seconds until set in the middle. Fold over and serve.

Selections per serving:
  1½ Fat
  2 Protein

Creamy Parsnip Soup

Serves 4
145 Calories per serving

This recipe is a good way of using old parsnips which sometimes have a hard central core running through them. Peel the parsnips, discard the hard core then weigh and proceed with the recipe.

1 onion

12oz (360g) parsnips

½ teaspoon ground coriander

½ pint (300ml) stock

1 tablespoon chopped parsley

12fl oz (360ml) skimmed milk

4 tablespoons single cream

½-1 teaspoon lemon juice

salt and pepper

a little carrot, grated

Selections per serving:
  ¾ Bread
  ¼ Milk
  ½ Vegetable
  55 Optional Calories

1 Chop the onion. Thinly slice the parsnips.

2 Place the onion in a container, cover and cook on HIGH for 2 minutes 30 seconds.

3 Stir the coriander, parsnips and ¼ pint (150ml) stock into the onion, add the parsley then cover and cook on HIGH for 9 minutes, or until the parsnips are cooked, stirring halfway through the cooking time.

4 Spoon the parsnip mixture into a food processor or liquidiser and process to a purée, add the remaining stock and milk.

5 Pour the parsnip purée into the container, cover and cook on HIGH for 4 minutes.

6 Stir the cream and lemon juice into the soup, cook for a further 40 seconds then leave to stand for 2 minutes.

7 Season with salt and pepper then ladle into soup bowls and garnish with a little grated carrot.

Eggs in a Creamy Cheese Sauce

Serves 2
285 Calories per serving

This dish is quick and simple to make. If you prefer, substitute fresh broccoli florets for frozen ones – just add 2 tablespoons water, cover and cook for about 5 minutes.

2 eggs

8oz (240g) frozen broccoli florets

1 tablespoon cornflour

¼ pint (150ml) skimmed milk

2oz (60g) soft cheese eg Blue Brie or Brie with herbs and peppercorns

Selections per serving:
¼ Milk
2 Protein
1¼ Vegetable
15 Optional Calories

1   Place the eggs in a saucepan, cover with cold water and leave for 10 minutes to hard-boil.

2   Place the broccoli in a container and cook according to the packaging instructions. Leave covered while cooking the sauce.

3   Place the cornflour in a bowl or jug, gradually blend in the milk and cook, uncovered, on HIGH for 2 minutes 30 seconds, stirring after the first minute and then every 30 seconds.

4   Cut the cheese into small pieces, add to the hot sauce and stir until melted.

5   Drain the broccoli and transfer to a serving dish or divide between two lipped plates. Shell the hard-boiled eggs, cut in half and arrange the eggs on top of the broccoli. Pour over the sauce and serve.

Creamy Potato Bake

Serves 4
115 Calories per serving

Serve this dish, with a selection of other vegetables, as an accompaniment to any main meal.

12oz (360g) potatoes

1 onion

1 small clove garlic

½ teaspoon chopped mint

4 teaspoons chopped parsley

4 tablespoons single cream

Selections per serving:
  1 Bread
  ¼ Vegetable
  50 Optional Calories

1 Thinly slice the potatoes.

2 Thinly slice the onion and finely chop the garlic.

3 Place the onion and garlic in a bowl, cover and cook on HIGH for 2 minutes 30 seconds, stir the mint and 3 teaspoons parsley into the mixture.

4 Layer the potato and onion mixture in a deep 6 inch (15cm) round container starting and ending with a layer of potatoes. Spoon the cream over the top then cover.

5 Cook on HIGH for 7 minutes 30 seconds. Leave to stand for 2 minutes, then test all the vegetables are cooked by inserting a skewer into the centre. Sprinkle with the remaining parsley and serve.

Vegetable Moussaka

Serves 4
295 Calories per serving
Serve this recipe with a mixed salad.

1 large aubergine

salt

2 onions

2 large sticks celery

1 tablespoon tomato purée

3 tablespoons stock or water

6oz (180g) drained canned sweetcorn

15oz (450g) baked beans in tomato sauce

9oz (270g) tofu

¼ teaspoon oregano

2 eggs

10fl oz (300ml) low-fat natural yogurt

½oz (15g) Parmesan cheese, finely grated

Selections per serving:
  ½ Bread
  ½ Milk
  2½ Protein
  1 Vegetable
  10 Optional Calories

1   Cut the aubergine into thin slices, about ¼ inch (6mm) thick. Sprinkle the aubergine liberally with salt and leave in a colander for about 30 minutes to allow the bitter juices to drip away.

2   Rinse the aubergine well under running cold water. Place the slices in a container, add 2 tablespoons water, cover and cook on HIGH for 4 minutes.

3   Roughly chop the onions and thickly slice the celery. Mix the tomato purée together with the stock or water. Transfer the onion and celery to a container and add the tomato purée and stock. Stir then cover and cook on HIGH for 5 minutes.

4   Stir the sweetcorn and baked beans into the hot onion and celery mixture.

5   Cut the tofu into ¾ inch (2cm) cubes and stir into the vegetable mixture, add the oregano then stir well. Cover the dish and microwave on HIGH for 6 minutes.

6   Drain the aubergine slices.

7   Make a thin layer of aubergines in a deep 6½ inch (17.5cm) dish then spoon over the bean and tofu mixture. Arrange the remaining slices of aubergine on top.

8   Whisk the eggs together with the yogurt and Parmesan cheese. Spoon the egg and yogurt mixture over the aubergine and cook, uncovered on MEDIUM for 12 minutes. Leave to stand for 5 minutes.

Egg and Spinach Supper

Serves 2
135 Calories per serving

If you are unable to obtain small spinach leaves, buy more than the weight given as all the coarse stalks must be removed.

12oz (360g) young spinach leaves

1 small onion, finely chopped

2 small cloves garlic, finely chopped

1 teaspoon tomato purée

¼ teaspoon chilli sauce

½ teaspoon vinegar

8oz (240g) canned chopped tomatoes

2 eggs

Selections per serving:
  1 Protein
  3½ Vegetable
  5 Optional Calories

1 Wash the spinach in several changes of water, shake the leaves to remove excess water then place in a dish, cover and cook on HIGH for 5 minutes 30 seconds. Leave to stand for 2 minutes then drain well, pressing out as much moisture as possible, and roughly chop the leaves.

2 Place the onion and garlic in a bowl, cover and cook on HIGH for 2 minutes.

3 Stir the tomato purée together with the chilli sauce, vinegar, tomatoes and chopped spinach, cover and cook on HIGH for 4 minutes until boiling.

4 Spoon the hot spinach and tomato sauce into two serving dishes. Make a dip in the centre of each dish and break one egg into each dish. Pierce the yolks with a cocktail stick.

5 Cover the dishes and cook on MEDIUM for 3 minutes. Leave to stand for 1 minute – 1 minute 30 seconds.

Parsnip Pudding

Serves 2 or 4
360 Calories per serving for 2
180 Calories per serving for 4

If you are particularly fond of parsnips this pudding makes a hearty supper dish which only requires a crisp salad to make a tasty meal. Alternatively serve it as a vegetable accompaniment for four people. Occasionally parsnips have rather 'woody' centres so weigh them after preparation.

1lb (480g) parsnips

½ tablespoon margarine

1 onion, finely chopped

6fl oz (180ml) skimmed milk

2 eggs

8oz (240g) quark-style cheese

nutmeg, freshly grated

salt and pepper

1   Roughy chop the parsnips.

2   Place the margarine and onion in a container, cover and cook on HIGH for 2 minutes.

3   Add the parsnips and 6 tablespoons milk to the onion, cover and cook on HIGH for 8 minutes, stirring halfway through the cooking time.

4   Mash the parsnip mixture. Beat the eggs with the remaining milk then beat the eggs and quark into the parsnip mixture. Season well with freshly grated nutmeg, salt and pepper.

5   Spoon the parsnip mixture into a 6-7 inch (15-17.5cm) round dish, cover and cook on HIGH for 6 minutes. Leave to stand for 5 minutes.

Selections per serving for 2:
    2 Bread
    ¾ Fat
    ¼ Milk
    3 Protein
    ½ Vegetable
    5 Optional Calories

Selections per serving for 4:
    1 Bread
    ¼ Fat
    1½ Protein
    ¼ Vegetable
    20 Optional Calories

Spanish Omelette

Serves 2
270 Calories per serving

This recipe makes an attractive, brightly coloured snack.

½ **onion**

½ **green pepper**

½ **red pepper**

3oz (90g) cooked potato

1 tablespoon margarine

2oz (60g) cooked peas

3 eggs

3 tablespoons skimmed milk

salt and pepper

1   Cut the onion, green and red peppers into slices to form semi-circles. Dice the cooked potato.

2   Place just over half the margarine in an 8 inch (20cm) flan dish and the remainder in a bowl.

3   Place the onion and peppers into the bowl, cover and cook on HIGH for 3 minutes.

4   Place the flan dish in the oven and cook uncovered, on HIGH for 30 seconds or until melted. Tilt the dish to spread the melted margarine over the base.

5   Spoon the onion and peppers evenly into the flan dish, add the potato and peas.

6   Lightly beat the eggs, milk and a little salt and pepper and pour over the vegetables.

7   Cook, uncovered, on HIGH for 1 minute 30 seconds, then stir round drawing the setting edge towards the centre so the runny centre runs towards the edge of the dish. Cook, uncovered, on HIGH for 1 minute and stir again. Lay a plate over the dish then cook on MEDIUM for 2 minutes. Leave to stand 2 minutes. If the centre of the omelette has not completely set after the standing time return to the oven for a few more seconds.

8   Slide the omelette out of the dish, cut in half and serve.

Selections per serving:
   ¾ Bread
   1½ Fat
   1½ Protein
   1 Vegetable
   5 Optional Calories

Baked Egg Custard

Serves 6
85 Calories per serving

Eggs should be cooked on a medium or low power to lessen the risk of overcooking and curdling. If your oven doesn't have a turntable turn the ramekins every few minutes.

---

1 pint (600ml) skimmed milk

few drops of vanilla essence

3 eggs

1½ tablespoons caster sugar

Selections per serving:
  ¼ Milk
  ½ Protein
  25 Optional Calories

1 Place the milk in a jug, add the vanilla essence and heat on HIGH for 4 minutes.

2 Whisk the eggs together with the sugar, pour over the hot milk and whisk once again. Strain the mixture then pour into six ramekins. Cover the ramekins with clingfilm and arrange in a circle in the oven.

3 Cook on MEDIUM for 3 minutes then reduce the heat to LOW for 9 minutes. Leave to stand for 5 minutes. The custard must be slightly wobbly in the centre when removed from the oven, it will set completely while standing. Do not overcook, the custards can always be returned to the oven for a short time if necessary.

Meringues

Makes 30
35 Calories per meringue

Microwave meringues differ from traditional meringues as they do not have the same texture or pale beige colour. Although they will keep quite well in an airtight container, they should be eaten fairly soon after baking as their texture becomes granular and sugary. This way of cooking is much quicker than the conventional method which can take several hours.

1 × size 5 egg white

9oz (270g) icing sugar

Selections per meringue:
35 Optional Calories

1   Break the egg white into a small bowl and whisk lightly with a fork.

2   Sieve the icing sugar then gradually whisk into the egg white to form a very stiff smooth mixture.

3   Line six muffin dishes or poached egg containers with paper cake cases and place 1 teaspoon of the mixture into each case. Cook, uncovered, on HIGH for 1 minute 15 seconds or until the meringue doesn't 'fall' when the power is off.

4   Carefully lift the meringues out of the muffin dishes then continue cooking the remaining mixture. The meringues may be removed from the paper cases while warm or cold.

Cheese Fondue

Serves 2 or 4
580 Calories per serving for 2
290 Calories per serving for 4

Serve this fondue as a main course for two people or as a starter for four.

6oz (180g) Gruyere cheese

1 tablespoon cornflour

1 clove garlic

4fl oz (120ml) white wine

3oz (90g) toasted French bread cut into 1 inch (2.5 cm) cubes

approximately 12oz (360g) selection of crudités such as cauliflower florets, carrot sticks, squares of pepper

1 Grate the cheese and mix it with the cornflour.

2 Cut the garlic in half and rub round the sides of the serving dish.

3 Pour the wine into the dish and place in the oven uncovered. Cook on HIGH for 1 minute.

4 Stir about half the cheese into the hot wine, cook on MEDIUM for 1 minute. Stir the wine mixture well then add the remaining cheese, stir and replace in the oven.

5 Cook the fondue on MEDIUM for 2-3 minutes, stirring every 30 seconds, until the mixture has combined.

6 Serve the fondue in the cooking dish with the toasted bread and crudités arranged on a separate plate. When the fondue cools and becomes stringy return to the oven and reheat on MEDIUM for 30-40 seconds.

Selections per serving for 2:
   1½ Bread
   3 Protein
   1½ Vegetable
   65 Optional Calories

Selections per serving for 4:
   ¾ Bread
   1½ Protein
   ¾ Vegetable
   30 Optional Calories

Honeycomb Pudding

Serves 6
90 Calories per serving

Serve this light pudding with a selection of fresh fruits; choose a variety of colours to make an attractive dessert.

2 large eggs, separated

1 pint (600ml) skimmed milk

few drops of vanilla essence

2 tablespoons sugar

few drops of yellow colouring (optional)

1½ tablespoons gelatine

pinch of cream of tartar

1   Place the egg yolks in a small bowl, add 2-3 tablespoons milk.

2   Place a further 2-3 tablespoons milk in a cup or small basin.

3   Pour the remaining milk into a bowl, add the vanilla and sugar and heat on HIGH for 2 minutes until warm.

4   Pour the warm milk onto the egg mixture, stirring all the time. Strain the mixture through a sieve into a clean bowl and return to the oven and cook on MEDIUM for about 4 minutes, stirring every 30 seconds. The egg yolks should be cooked but the mixture must not boil. Add a little yellow colouring if desired.

5   Place the cup or small bowl containing a little milk in the oven and heat on HIGH for 40 seconds, sprinkle the gelatine into the hot milk and stir well until completely dissolved. If necessary return to the oven for a few more seconds. Stir the dissolved gelatine into the egg and milk and leave until cool.

6   Whisk the egg whites with the cream of tartar until peaking then fold gently but thoroughly through the cool custard. Spoon into a pretty serving dish or mould.

7   Either serve the Honeycomb Pudding directly from the bowl or just before serving turn the mould out on to a plate and serve with fresh fruit.

Selections per serving:
  ¼ Milk
  ¼ Protein
  35 Optional Calories

Chocolate Chestnut Pudding

Serves 4
225 Calories per serving

This pudding makes a rich dessert suitable for a family dinner or an elaborate dinner party.

½oz (15g) cornflour

2 tablespoons cocoa

2 tablespoons sugar

½ pint (300ml) skimmed milk

6oz (180g) chestnut purée

6oz (180g) drained canned apricots

2 eggs, lightly beaten

¼ teaspoon icing sugar

Selections per serving:
  ½ Bread
  ¼ Fruit
  ¼ Milk
  ½ Protein
  65 Optional Calories

1 Blend the cornflour, cocoa and sugar together with the milk. Place in the oven and cook, uncovered, on HIGH for 4 minutes, stirring every 1 minute – 1 minute 30 seconds.

2 Gradually blend the chocolate sauce into the chestnut purée.

3 Roughly chop the apricots and divide between four large ramekins or serving dishes.

4 Stir the beaten eggs into the chocolate and chestnut mixture then spoon on top of the apricots. Cover the ramekins and cook on MEDIUM for 6 minutes then LOW for 6 minutes. They should be slightly wobbly in the middle.

5 Leave the puddings to stand for 2 minutes, if they have not completely set return to the oven and cook on LOW for a short time. Leave until cold.

6 Just before serving dust the tops of the puddings with the icing sugar.

Tropical Cheesecake

Serves 10
195 Calories per serving

Don't add any additional sweetener to the cheesecake. The sugar present in the biscuit base, fruits and chocolate is sufficient to sweeten the mixture and enhance the full flavour of the fruits.

4 tablespoons margarine

8 large digestive biscuits, made into crumbs

1 medium mango

6oz (180g) curd cheese

6oz (180g) fromage frais

1 medium orange

1½ tablespoons gelatine

2 large egg whites

pinch of cream of tartar

2 fresh figs

1 kiwi fruit

1oz (30g) chocolate, grated or made into curls

Selections per serving:
  ¾ Bread
  1 Fat
  ½ Fruit
  ½ Protein
  40 Optional Calories

1 Measure the margarine into a bowl, microwave on HIGH for 1 minute until melted, stir the biscuit crumbs into the margarine and mix well. Press the mixture into the base of an 8 inch (20cm) springform tin.

2 Cut the mango in half, scoop the flesh from each half and remove all the flesh attached to the stone. Place the mango, curd cheese and fromage frais in a liquidiser or food processor and process to a purée.

3 Squeeze the juice from the orange, place about half in a cup, stir in the gelatine. Heat on HIGH for 60 seconds, stir well and leave until the gelatine has dissolved. Mix the remaining orange juice into the curd cheese mixture.

4 Pour the dissolved gelatine into the curd cheese purée and process once again. Pour the purée into a bowl and leave until thick and beginning to set.

5 Whisk the egg whites with the cream of tartar until peaking, fold into the setting mixture and spoon over the top of the biscuit base. Leave until completely set.

6 Just before serving, carefully remove the cheesecake from the tin and slide onto a flat serving plate. Thinly slice the figs and kiwi fruit. Arrange the fruit on top of the cheesecake and spill the grated chocolate onto the centre.

Citrus Flan

Serves 8
260 Calories per serving

The lime and lemon give this flan a real tang – if you wish substitute the mandarins with fresh or drained canned cherries.

1 × 8 inch (20cm) cooked flan case (see page 219)

1 lime

1 lemon

2 eggs

1oz (30g) cornflour

1½oz (45g) caster sugar

8oz (240g) curd cheese

4fl oz (120ml) skimmed milk

4oz (120g) well-drained canned mandarins

Selections per serving:
    ¾ Bread
    1½ Fat
    ¾ Protein
    55 Optional Calories

1   Place the pastry case on a serving plate.

2   Finely grate the zest of the lime, place in a large jug or bowl. Squeeze the juice from the lime and lemon – there should be about 5 tablespoons of juice in all.

3   Lightly beat the eggs.

4   Place the cornflour and sugar in the bowl with the lime zest. Gradually stir in the fruit juice then whisk in the curd cheese and finally the eggs.

5   Heat the milk on HIGH for 1 minute 30 seconds, pour into the curd cheese mixture then spoon into the pastry case.

6   Cook the flan on MEDIUM for 5 minutes then reduce the power to LOW and cook for a further 5 minutes. The centre of the flan should still be wobbly. Leave to stand for 6-7 minutes. If necessary return the flan to the oven and cook on LOW for a short time, checking every 20 seconds.

7   Leave the flan to cool, then decorate with the mandarins and serve.

Banana Chocolate Sundae

Serves 4
115 Calories per serving

The rum in the banana and chocolate sauce may be replaced by a few drops of vanilla essence. This would reduce the calorie count by 10 Calories per serving.

½oz (15g) cornflour

2 tablespoons cocoa

½ pint (300ml) skimmed milk

2 medium bananas

1 tablespoon rum

artificial sweetener

1 sachet gelatine

1 egg white

pinch of cream of tartar

1 Place the cornflour and cocoa in a bowl. Reserve 3 tablespoons milk then gradually blend the remainder into the cornflour mixture.

2 Place the bowl in the oven and cook, uncovered, on HIGH for 1 minute 30 seconds, stir well then continue cooking on HIGH for 2 minutes, stirring every 30-40 seconds until the sauce is smooth and thick.

3 Pour the sauce into a liquidiser, add the bananas and rum and process. Sweeten to taste with artificial sweetener.

4 Pour the reserved milk into a cup or small basin, sprinkle in the gelatine and stir well. Heat the milk and gelatine on HIGH for 45 seconds, stir round until the gelatine has dissolved – if necessary return to the microwave for 5-10 seconds.

5 Stir the dissolved gelatine into the sauce. Pour into a bowl, lay a sheet of damp greaseproof paper on the sauce to prevent a skin forming as it cools.

6 When the sauce is cool and has begun to set, whisk the egg white together with the cream of tartar until peaking.

7 Gently fold the egg white through the sauce then spoon into four serving dishes or glasses. Chill until completely set.

Selections per serving:
  1 Fruit
  ¼ Milk
  40 Optional Calories

Banana Crisp

Serves 4
205 Calories per serving

This dessert is particularly popular with children. Serve it immediately after baking or the crisp topping will absorb moisture from the custard base.

---

1 pint (600ml) skimmed milk

1½oz (45g) custard powder

¼ teaspoon instant coffee powder (optional)

3 medium bananas

artificial sweetener

1 tablespoon golden syrup

1½oz (45g) cornflakes

Selections per serving:
  ¼ Bread
  1½ Fruit
  ½ Milk
  50 Optional Calories

1   Blend the milk together with the custard powder and coffee powder. Cook, uncovered, on HIGH for about 7 minutes until boiling and very thick. Stir every minute.

2   Remove the boiling custard from the oven.

3   Slice the bananas and stir into the custard, sweeten to taste with artificial sweetener.

4   Spoon the banana custard into a serving dish.

5   Heat the golden syrup on HIGH for 50 seconds, stir in the cornflakes and mix well – don't worry the syrup won't completely coat the flakes.

6   Spoon the cornflakes over the custard and return to the oven. Cook, uncovered, on HIGH for 1 minute. Leave to stand for 3 minutes.

Grains and Pulses

Very little time can be saved by cooking grains and pulses in a microwave oven as they require time to rehydrate. The total time, including cooking and standing is about the same as cooking on the hob and can be even longer with large quantities.

PULSES

Split lentils and peas are the only pulses which don't require soaking prior to cooking. Many beans such as kidney, haricot and soya must be soaked and then boiled rapidly for 10 minutes in order to destroy harmful toxins. It is possible to do this in the microwave but it is easier on the hob. The time to cook pulses is considerable, for example 4oz (120g) split peas should be cooked on HIGH for 7 minutes then LOW for about 25 minutes followed by a standing time of 5-6 minutes. The time is reduced considerably by using a pressure cooker. However the two methods of cooking on the hob and in a microwave may be combined with the initial boiling carried out on the hob then completed in the microwave. The advantage of this method is that cooking will stop automatically after a set time.

GRAINS

There are many different grains and it would be impossible to cover them all in such a limited space.

The following guidelines should be used for grains which are to be served as a vegetable acompaniment in the place of potatoes. If a softer grain is required, for example when making patties or vegetable burgers, cook in a little more water and for a longer time.

Use a large container to allow plenty of room for boiling up.

Add salt after cooking.

Cover with a lid or pierced clingfilm.

Add a little oil to keep the grains separate.

Remove from the oven while still a little firm to bite then allow cooking to be completed during the standing time.

Cooking Guidelines for Grains
The following quantities of grains and liquid should result in the water being absorbed and the grains remaining separate.

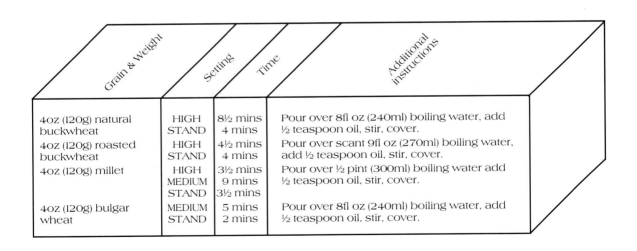

Grain & Weight	Setting	Time	Additional instructions
4oz (120g) natural buckwheat	HIGH STAND	8½ mins 4 mins	Pour over 8fl oz (240ml) boiling water, add ½ teaspoon oil, stir, cover.
4oz (120g) roasted buckwheat	HIGH STAND	4½ mins 4 mins	Pour over scant 9fl oz (270ml) boiling water, add ½ teaspoon oil, stir, cover.
4oz (120g) millet	HIGH MEDIUM STAND	3½ mins 9 mins 3½ mins	Pour over ½ pint (300ml) boiling water add ½ teaspoon oil, stir, cover.
4oz (120g) bulgar wheat	MEDIUM STAND	5 mins 2 mins	Pour over 8fl oz (240ml) boiling water, add ½ teaspoon oil, stir, cover.

Rice

Although very little time is saved cooking even small quantities of rice, the microwave does cook it well. It is frequently more convenient as there is less risk of overcooking and it will not stick to the base of the container – unlike cooking in a saucepan when a sticky layer often forms over the base and results in burning. A mirowave is particularly useful for reheating rice – because it doesn't require any additional liquid, the grains remain fluffy and separate: just cover and reheat.

The following guidelines should be used:

Always cook in a deep container as the water boils and rises considerably.

Boiling water or stock speeds up the cooking time. Add a little oil to keep the cooked grains fluffy and separate even after the standing time.

Cover the container with a lid or pierced clingfilm so a little steam can escape during cooking.

Add salt after cooking.

Remove the rice from the oven while undercooked. During the standing time cooking will continue and the liquid should be completely absorbed.

Cooking Guidelines for Rice

Below is a chart for cooking different varieties of rice. I always soak basmati rice before cooking as I consider the fine flavour of the rice makes it worthy of extra attention. Although it isn't absolutely essential, by soaking in salted water the starch surrounding each grain is removed and this helps to prevent the grains sticking.

Rice & Weight	Setting	Time	Additional instructions
4oz (120g) easy-cook white long grain rice	HIGH STAND	6½ mins 5 mins	Pour over 8fl oz (240ml) boiling water, add ½ teaspoon oil, stir, cover.
4oz (120g) easy-cook brown long grain rice	HIGH MEDIUM STAND	5 mins 13 mins 5 mins	
4oz (120g) white long grain rice (not easy-cook)	HIGH STAND	7 mins 6 mins	
4oz (120g) wholegrain long grain rice (not easy-cook)	HIGH MEDIUM STAND	5 mins 16 mins 6 mins	Pour over ½ pint (300ml) boiling water, add ½ teaspoon oil, stir, cover.
4oz (120g) white basmati rice	HIGH STAND	5 mins 5 mins	Soak in cold salted water for 25-30 mins, drain, rinse well, pour over 8fl oz (240ml) boiling water, add ½ teaspoon oil, stir, cover.
4oz (120g) brown basmati rice	HIGH MEDIUM STAND	6 mins 12 mins 5 mins	Soak in cold salted water for 25-30 mins, drain, rinse well, pour over ½ pint (300ml) boiling water, add ½ teaspoon oil, stir, cover.
4oz (120g) wild rice	HIGH MEDIUM STAND	3 mins 45 mins 8 mins	Pour over ¾ pint (450ml) boiling water, add ½ teaspoon oil, stir, cover.

Basic Boiled Rice

Serves 2
205 Calories per serving

This recipe gives two large helpings, if you wish to increase the numbers of servings alter the Selections and calorie counts as necessary.

4oz (120g) easy-cook long grain rice

8fl oz (240ml) boiling water

½ teaspoon oil

salt

1 Place the rice in a deep container, add the boiling water and oil.

2 Stir the rice and water, cover with a lid or pierced clingfilm.

3 Cook on HIGH for 6 minutes 30 seconds, leave to stand for 5 minutes – the water should have been completely absorbed.

4 Fluff up the grains of rice with a fork and serve or add a little salt, stir then serve.

Selections per serving:
  2 Bread
  ¼ Fat

Simple Savoury Rice
While the rice is standing cook 4oz (120g) frozen vegetables, covered but without additional water, on HIGH for 4 minutes. Stir halfway through the cooking time, then mix the hot rice together with the vegetables and season with salt.
240 Calories per serving
Selections per serving:
2 Bread
¼ Fat
½ Vegetable

Rice with Herbs
Add finely grated zest of ½ lemon, 1-2 tablespoons finely chopped parsley before standing time.
225 Calories per serving
Selections per serving:
2 Bread
¼ Fat

Nutty Rice
Place 1 teaspoon margarine in a bowl, add ½ finely chopped onion and ½ finely chopped red pepper, cover and cook on HIGH for 2 minutes, add to the hot rice with 1oz (30g) finely chopped walnuts.
340 Calories per serving
Selections per serving:
2 Bread
1 Fat
1 Protein
½ Vegetable
10 Optional Calories

PASTA

Cooking pasta in the microwave has the same drawbacks as rice, it takes time to rehydrate and consequently very little time is saved. It can however be extremely convenient.

The following guidelines should be followed:

Always cook in a deep container to allow plenty of room for the liquid to boil high; it boils higher than rice.

Always add boiling water – salt may be added if desired.

Add a little oil to keep the pasta separate even after standing.

Stir the pasta and boiling water before cooking and ensure the level of liquid is ½ inch (1.25cm) or more above the pasta – spaghetti should be broken in two, if it stands above the water it will harden.

Cover the container with a lid or pierced clingfilm so a little steam can escape during cooking.

Remove the pasta from the oven before it is completely cooked, as cooking will continue after the power has been turned off during the standing time.

Cooking Guidelines for Pasta

Use the following as a guide but add about 1 minute 30 seconds – 2 minutes if using wholewheat pasta. All the weights are for dried pasta unless otherwise specified.

Pasta & Weight	Setting	Time	Additional instructions
8oz (240g) fresh spaghetti	HIGH STAND	3½ mins 2 mins	Pour over 1½ pints (900ml) boiling water, add 1 teaspoon oil, ¼ teaspoon salt, stir, cover.
4oz (120g) spaghetti	HIGH STAND	7 mins 5 mins	
4oz (120g) fresh tagliatelle	HIGH STAND	2½ mins 2 mins	Pour over 1½ pints (900ml) boiling water, add 1 teaspoon oil, ¼ teaspoon salt, stir, cover.
4oz (120g) tagliatelle	HIGH STAND	3 mins 5 mins	
4oz (120g) large pasta shapes (approx 20 large shells)	HIGH STAND	8 mins 7 mins	Pour over 1½ pints (900ml) boiling water, add 1 teaspoon oil, ¼ teaspoon salt, stir, cover.
4oz (120g) macaroni	HIGH STAND	6½ mins 5 mins	Pour over 1¼ pints (750ml) boiling water, add 1 teaspoon oil, ¼ teaspoon salt, stir, cover.
4oz (120g) quick-cook macaroni	HIGH STAND	3 mins 4 mins	Pour over 1¼ pints (750ml) boiling water, add 1 teaspoon oil, ¼ teaspoon salt, stir, cover.
4oz (120g) small pasta shapes eg bows	HIGH STAND	5 mins 5 mins	

Bean and Barley Soup

Serves 4
140 Calories per serving

Usually pearl barley is added to stews or casseroles which are cooked for a long time. This recipe takes about 30 minutes to cook, quicker than it would take simmering on the hob. A 15½oz (439g) can butter beans contains the amount of drained beans required for this recipe.

1 small clove garlic

1 onion

½ green pepper, seeded

2oz (60g) pearl barley

½ teaspoon marjoram

½ teaspoon mild chilli powder

8oz (240g) drained canned butter beans

14oz (440g) can chopped tomatoes

18fl oz (540ml) hot stock

1 Finely chop the garlic, onion and green pepper. Place in a suitable container, cover and cook on HIGH for 3 minutes 30 seconds.

2 Rinse the pearl barley then stir into the onion mixture together with the marjoram and chilli powder. Mix in the butter beans, chopped tomatoes and hot stock.

3 Cover the container with a lid or with a piece of clingfilm pulled slightly away at one side to enable the soup to be stirred occasionally.

4 Cook on HIGH for 12 minutes then stir and cook on MEDIUM for 20 minutes. Stir two or three times during the cooking time.

5 Leave to stand 3-4 minutes then ladle into soup bowls and serve.

Selections per serving:
   1 Bread
   1½ Vegetable
   15 Optional Calories

Lentil Soup

Serves 4
120 Calories per serving

This soup is particularly welcome on a cold chilly night. To make it into a hearty snack add some frozen vegetables to the processed soup, cover and cook for a few minutes until the vegetables are cooked.

1 onion

1 carrot

1-2 sticks celery

14oz (420g) can tomatoes

12fl oz (360ml) boiling stock

4oz (120g) split red lentils

salt and pepper

Selections per serving:
  1 Bread
  2 Vegetable

1 Chop the onion, carrot and celery.

2 Place the prepared vegetables in a container, cover and cook on HIGH for 4 minutes.

3 Stir in the tomatoes, stock and lentils. Stir the lentil mixture well, breaking up the whole tomatoes.

4 Cover the container and cook on HIGH for 13 minutes.

5 Leave to stand for 4 minutes then spoon into a food processor or liquidiser and process to a purée.

6 Season the soup with salt and pepper then reheat – the time for reheating the soup will obviously depend on the starting temperature.

Basic Boiled Spaghetti

Serves 2
210 Calories per serving

4oz (120g) spaghetti

1¼ pints (900ml) boiling water

¼ teaspoon salt

1 teaspoon oil

Selections per serving:
  2 Bread
  ½ Fat

1   Break the spaghetti into 5-6 inch (12.5-15cm) lengths, place in a container.

2   Pour the boiling water into the container. As the ends soften, gently press the pasta into the boiling water until they are completely submerged.

3   Stir the salt and oil into the container.

4   Cover the container with a lid or pierced clingfilm.

5   Cook on HIGH for 7 minutes, leave to stand for 5 minutes then drain and serve.

VARIATION

Buttered Spaghetti:

245 Calories per serving
Add 1 tablespoon butter to the drained spaghetti, toss well then sprinkle with 1 teaspoon chopped parsley.
Selections per serving:
2 Bread
½ Fat
50 Optional Calories

Spaghetti with Artichokes

Serves 4
245 Calories per serving

Serve this recipe with a crisp mixed salad.

6oz (180g) spaghetti

1 teaspoon oil

¼ teaspoon salt

3oz (90g) curd cheese

3 tablespoons single cream

14oz (400g) can artichoke bottoms

2-3 teaspoons chopped chervil

paprika

Selections per serving:
  1½ Bread
  ¼ Fat
  ¼ Protein
  1¼ Vegetable
  45 Optional Calories

1 Place the spaghetti in a large container, pour over 1½ pints (900ml) boiling water, add the oil and salt, cover and cook on HIGH for 8 minutes, leave to stand for 5 minutes.

2 While the spaghetti is cooking, gradually blend the curd cheese and cream together in a bowl.

3 Drain the artichokes and cut each of the artichoke bottoms into four. Stir the chervil and artichokes into the curd cheese mixture and cover the bowl.

4 While the spaghetti is standing place the curd cheese mixture in the oven and cook on LOW for 3 minutes.

5 Drain the spaghetti, add the curd cheese mixture and stir well.

6 Spoon the spaghetti into a serving dish or divide between four serving bowls and sprinkle over a little paprika.

Lentil Lasagne

Serves 4
590 Calories per serving

This recipe comprises layers of lasagne and lentil sauce with a mixture of cauliflower cheese in the centre. I could only find lasagne labelled 'no need to soak' but I still gave it a preliminary boil.

1 large clove garlic, finely chopped

1 onion, finely chopped

1 red pepper, seeded and finely chopped

14oz (440g) can chopped tomatoes

6oz (180g) split red lentils

½ pint (300ml) water

½ teaspoon oregano

½ teaspoon yeast extract

8oz (240g) cauliflower florets

6oz (180g) lasagne (about 8 sheets)

1 teaspoon oil

¼ teaspoon salt

2oz (60g) cornflour

1½ pints (900ml) skimmed milk

4oz (120g) cheese, grated

1 Place the garlic, onion and red pepper in a container or bowl, cover and cook on HIGH for 4 minutes.

2 Stir the tomatoes, lentils, water and oregano into the onion mixture, cover and cook on HIGH for 16-17 minutes until the lentils are cooked. Stir in the yeast extract. Leave covered while completing the remaining recipe.

3 Roughly chop the cauliflower florets, place in a container with 2 tablespoons water, cover and cook on HIGH for 4 minutes 30 seconds.

4 Lay the lasagne in a flat dish, pour over 1½ pints (900ml) boiling water, add the oil and salt and cover the dish with pierced clingfilm. Cook on HIGH for 5 minutes, Leave to stand for 4-5 minutes.

5 Blend the cornflour to a paste with a little milk. Pour the remaining milk into a bowl or suitable container and heat, uncovered, on HIGH for 6 minutes. Stir in the cornflour paste and mix well. Return to the oven and cook on HIGH for 6 minutes until boiling and thick. Reserve about ½oz (15g) cheese and stir the remainder into the hot sauce.

6 Return the lentil mixture to the oven and reheat for 3 minutes or until steaming.

7   While the lentil sauce is reheating drain and separate the sheets of lasagne and spread about one third of the cheese sauce over the base of a rectangular dish (about 9 × 7 inch/22.5×17.5cm). Arrange two sheets of lasagne on top of the sauce.

8   Spoon half the lentil mixture over the lasagne and level the surface with the back of a spoon. Cover the lentil mixture with two sheets of lasagne and scatter the cauliflower over, then pour just under half of the remaining cheese sauce evenly over.

9   Arrange two more sheets of lasagne on the cheese sauce and repeat with a layer of the remaining lentil mixture and sheet of lasagne. Pour the rest of the cheese sauce over and sprinkle with the reserved grated cheese.

10   Return the completed Lentil Lasagne to the oven and cook, uncovered, on HIGH for 4 minutes until bubbling.

Selections per serving:
   2 Bread
   ¼ Fat
   ¾ Milk
   2½ Protein
   2½ Vegetable

Peppered Spaghetti

Serves 4
270 Calories per serving

Use two forks to lift and transfer the Peppered Spaghetti from the cooking dish to the serving plates: this will help to separate the strands of pasta.

3 medium peppers – use a variety of colours

2 teaspoons margarine

1½ teaspoons finely chopped chilli

4oz (120g) curd cheese

6oz (180g) wholewheat spaghetti

¼ teaspoon salt

1 teaspoon oil

Selections per serving:
  1½ Bread
  ¾ Fat
  ½ Protein
  1½ Vegetable

1 Remove the core and seeds from the peppers, cut into small dice.

2 Place the margarine and chilli in a container, cover and cook on HIGH for 1 minute.

3 Add the peppers to the chilli and stir well, cover and cook on HIGH for 6 minutes.

4 Stir the curd cheese into the peppers and leave to stand.

5 Break the spaghetti in half and place in a container, pour over the boiling water and add the salt and oil.

6 Cover the container and cook on HIGH for 9 minutes, leave to stand for 6 minutes then drain.

7 Stir the curd cheese and peppers into the hot drained spaghetti and return to the oven. Cook on HIGH for 1 minute, stir well then add a little extra salt and serve.

Blue Cheese Tagliatelle

Serves 2
430 Calories per serving

Fresh tagliatelle is now available in many supermarkets, when it is cooked it doubles in weight. If you wish to use the dried variety substitute 4oz (120g) dried tagliatelle.

6oz (180g) fresh tagliatelle

1 teaspoon oil

salt

2oz (60g) blue cheese, eg Danish Blue

2oz (60g) fromage frais

½ medium apple

1 Place the tagliatelle in a large container, add 1¼ pints (750ml) boiling water, the oil and ¼ teaspoon salt. Cover with a lid or pierced clingfilm and cook on HIGH for 3 minutes, leave to stand for 4 minutes then drain well.

2 While the pasta is cooking, crumble the blue cheese into a bowl, then stir in the fromage frais.

3 Cut the apple in half and remove the core then cut into small dice.

4 Stir the cheese mixture through the hot tagliatelle, add the apple and mix well. Serve hot.

VARIATION
Add ½oz (15g) roughly chopped peanuts.

Selections per serving:
   2 Bread
   ¾ Fat
   ¼ Fruit
   2 Protein
   445 Calories per serving for this variation

Selections per serving:
   2 Bread
   ½ Fat
   ¼ Fruit
   1½ Protein

Stuffed Peppers

Serves 4
245 Calories per serving

Choose peppers which are fairly flat at each end and that will stand upright. The cooking time will vary according to the firmness and size of the peppers.

4 medium peppers – red, yellow, green, orange or a mixture

1 onion

4oz (120g) bulgar wheat

8fl oz (240ml) boiling vegetable stock

1oz (30g) sultanas

1oz (30g) cashew nut kernels

1 teaspoon pumpkin seeds

¼ teaspoon thyme

½oz (15g) cheese, finely grated

Selections per serving:
  1 Bread
  ¼ Fat
  ¼ Fruit
  ½ Protein
  1½ Vegetable
  15 Optional Calories

1 Cut a ½ inch (1.25cm) slice from the top of each pepper. Cut the cores out of the peppers and discard the seeds. Finely chop the pepper slices.

2 Finely chop the onion and place in a dish together with the chopped pepper.

3 Cover the onion mixture and cook on HIGH for 3 minutes.

4 Stir the bulgar wheat and boiling stock into the onion mixture, cover and cook on MEDIUM for 5 minutes, then leave to stand for 2 minutes.

5 Place the sultanas, cashew nut kernels and pumpkin seeds on a chopping board and chop them together finely. Stir the chopped mixture, together with the thyme and grated cheese, into the bulgar wheat. Spoon the stuffing into the peppers and place in a circle in a container.

6 Pour 4fl oz (120ml) cold water round the peppers, cover and cook on HIGH for 8-10 minutes giving a quarter turn twice during the cooking time. Leave to stand for 3 minutes.

Vegetarian Polenta

Serves 4
455 Calories per serving

Polenta flour is a fine maize flour but you can substitute coarse cornmeal or maize flour if you prefer.

1 pint (600ml) skimmed milk

4oz (120g) polenta flour

2 eggs, lightly beaten

1 onion

1 large green pepper

¾-1 teaspoon finely chopped chilli

4oz (120g) mushrooms

½ teaspoon turmeric

6oz (180g) green lentils

6oz (180g) cooked or drained canned chick peas

1 tablespoon tomato purée

18fl oz (540ml) vegetable stock

2 teaspoons Worcestershire sauce

1   Pour the milk into a large bowl, microwave on HIGH for 6 minutes. Sprinkle the flour into the boiling milk, stirring all the time. Return to the oven and cook, uncovered, on HIGH for 4 minutes 30 seconds, stirring frequently until the mixture is very thick. Allow to cool for about 4 minutes.

2   Stir the eggs into the hot mixture. Cook on LOW for 1 minute 30 seconds, stirring every 30 seconds.

3   Line a shallow dish about 8 × 6 inches (20×15cm) with non-stick baking parchment.

4   Spoon the thick milk mixture into the dish and level the surface with the back of a spoon. If the mixture sticks to the spoon rinse it under cold water then shake to remove excess water and continue. Chill for 3-4 hours.

5   Slice the onion and green pepper, place in a container together with the chilli, cover and microwave on HIGH for 2 minutes.

6   Slice or roughly chop the mushrooms and add to the onion and peppers. Stir the turmeric, lentils and chick peas into the bowl.

7   Mix the tomato purée together with the stock and Worcesteshire sauce, cover and cook on HIGH for 10 minutes then reduce the power and cook on LOW for 20 minutes.

8   Turn the polenta mixture onto a work surface and cut into sixteen triangles. Arrange the triangles round the edge of a square or rectangular serving dish. Spoon the hot lentil mixture into the centre, cover and cook on HIGH for 2 minutes. Leave to stand for 5 minutes.

Selections per serving:
  1 Bread
  ½ Milk
  2½ Protein
  1 Vegetable
  5 Optional Calories

Mushroom Risotto

Serves 2
295 Calories per serving

Use the large flat mushrooms for this dish, they have a stronger flavour than button mushrooms. If you are in a hurry substitute white easy-cook rice, add 8fl oz (240ml) boiling vegetable stock and cook for 6 minutes 30 seconds.

2 teaspoons olive oil

1 large onion, finely chopped

1 clove garlic, finely chopped

6oz (180g) mushrooms, roughly chopped

½ teaspoon coriander seeds, crushed

4oz (120g) long grain brown rice

½ pint (300ml) boiling vegetable stock

1   Place the oil, onion, garlic, mushrooms and coriander in a dish, cover and cook on HIGH for 4 minutes 30 seconds.

2   Stir the rice into the hot vegetables, pour the boiling stock into the dish, stir well then cover and cook on HIGH for 20 minutes stirring twice during the cooking time.

3   Leave to stand for 6-7 minutes.

Selections per serving:
  2 Bread
  1 Fat
  2 Vegetable

Shell Salad

Serves 4
295 Calories per serving

A large fresh red pepper may be used in place of the pimento. Grill the fresh pepper under a very hot heat until black and charred all over, plunge into cold water then peel off the skin and remove the core and seeds.

20 large pasta shells – about 4oz (120g)

1 teaspoon oil

salt

8oz (240g) curd cheese

4oz (120g) fromage frais

1 large canned pimento

2oz (60g) lean cooked smoked ham

pepper sauce

shredded lettuce

Selections per serving:
  1 Bread
  ¼ Fat
  2 Protein
  ¼ Vegetable

1 Place the pasta in a large container, add 1½ pints (900ml) boiling water, the oil and ¼ teaspoon salt – the water should be about ¾ inch (2cm) above the level of the pasta.

2 Cover the container with a lid or a pierced piece of clingfilm and cook on HIGH for 8 minutes. Leave to stand for 7 minutes then drain well.

3 Mash the curd cheese together with the fromage frais.

4 Finely chop the pimento and ham.

5 Stir the pimento and ham into the cheese mixture. Season to taste with pepper sauce and salt.

6 Using a teaspoon, carefully stuff the pasta shells with the ham and cheese stuffing.

7 Arrange the pasta shells on a bed of shredded lettuce.

Vegetable and Rice Bake

Serves 4
275 Calories per serving

If the rice has been cooked in the microwave with additional oil remember to add the number of Selections or calories to every serving.

2 onions

1 head fennel

15oz (440g) can chopped tomatoes

¼ teaspoon basil

1-1½ teaspoons Worcestershire sauce

1oz (30g) cornflour

¾ pint (450ml) skimmed milk

9oz (270g) cooked long grain rice

3oz (90g) cheese, grated

salt and pepper

1. Finely slice the onions and fennel, place in a container and stir in 4-5 tablespoons of the juice from the can of tomatoes.

2. Cover the onion mixture and cook on HIGH for 5 minutes.

3. Stir the chopped tomatoes, basil and 1 teaspoon Worcestershire sauce into the onion mixture, cover and return to the oven. Cook on HIGH for 5 minutes then on MEDIUM for 15 minutes, stirring three or four times during cooking. The mixture should be fairly thick.

4. Gradually blend the cornflour together with the milk, cook on HIGH for 5 minutes, stirring frequently, until boiling and thickened.

5. Stir the rice and cheese into the sauce.

6. Season the tomato mixture well with salt and pepper and add a little more Worcestershire sauce if desired.

7. Spoon about one-third of the rice sauce into a small deep dish. Spoon the tomato mixture on top and cover with the remaining rice sauce.

8. Place the Vegetable and Rice Bake in the oven and cook, uncovered, on HIGH for 3 minutes, then leave to stand for 3 minutes.

Selections per serving:
  1 Bread
  ¼ Milk
  ¾ Protein
  3 Vegetable
  10 Optional Calories

Kedgeree

Serves 2
385 Calories per serving

Other varieties of rice may be used instead of the easy-cook white, refer to the chart on page 113 for the recommended cooking times.

4oz (120g) easy-cook long grain rice

8fl oz (240ml) boiling water

1 teaspoon oil

6oz (180g) smoked cod

1 hard-boiled egg

2 teaspoons chopped chives

1 tablespoon chopped parsley

1 egg, beaten

Selections per serving:
  2 Bread
  ½ Fat
  3½ Protein

1   Place the rice in a container, stir in the boiling water and oil then cover and cook on HIGH for 6 minutes 30 seconds. Leave to stand for 5 minutes.

2   Place the smoked cod on a lipped plate and cover tightly with pierced clingfilm. The clingfilm should not be in contact with the fish.

3   Cook on HIGH for 2 minutes, leave to stand for 1 minute then flake the cod into large pieces and discard the skin.

4   Finely chop the hard-boiled egg.

5   Stir the cod, hard-boiled egg and herbs into the hot rice, stir in the beaten egg, cover and cook on HIGH for 30 seconds.

6   Leave to stand for 4 minutes then fluff the rice up with a fork and serve.

Rice and Pea Salad

Serves 4
350 Calories per serving

Basmati rice gives this salad a delicious, slightly nutty flavour.

4oz (120g) green split peas

4oz (120g) white basmati rice

salt

5 teaspoons olive oil

1 teaspoon wine vinegar

1 clove garlic, crushed

pepper

1. Rinse the split peas, place in a container and add ½ pint (300ml) boiling water, cover and cook on HIGH for 7 minutes. Reduce the heat to LOW and cook for 25 minutes or until all the water has been absorbed and the peas are tender but not soft. Leave to stand for 5 minutes.

2. Rinse the rice, place in a bowl and cover with plenty of water, stir in 1 teaspoon salt and leave for 25-30 minutes. Drain and rinse well under running cold water.

3. Place the rice in a container, add 8fl oz (240ml) boiling water and 1 teaspoon oil, cover and cook on HIGH for 5 minutes, fluff up the grains, then cover and leave to stand for 5 minutes.

4. Mix the split peas together with the rice.

5. Place the vinegar and remaining oil in a small cup or basin, add the garlic and whisk together with a little salt and pepper. Pour the dressing over the peas and rice and leave until cool, fluff up the salad and leave until cold.

Selections per serving:
  2 Bread
  1¼ Fat

Peanut Pasta Salad

Serves 2
260 Calories per serving

Serve this dish as soon as it is cooked otherwise the peanut dressing will cool
and stick the pasta shapes together.

2oz (60g) pasta bows or spirals

¾ pint (450ml) boiling water

¼ teaspoon salt

1 teaspoon oil

2oz (60g) tiny broccoli florets

2 tablespoons peanut butter

2 tablespoons skimmed milk

½oz (15g) raisins

1   Place the pasta in a large container, pour
    over the boiling water and add the salt
    and oil – the water should be about
    ¾ inch (2cm) above the level of the
    pasta.

2   Cook on HIGH for 6 minutes, stand for
    5 minutes then drain well.

3   While the pasta is standing, place the
    broccoli florets in a container, add
    2 tablespoons water, then cover and
    cook on HIGH for 2 minutes.

4   Place the peanut butter in a bowl and
    gradually blend in the milk.

5   Drain the broccoli and then stir into the
    peanut butter dressing.

6   Drain the pasta then add to the dressing
    together with the raisins. Mix well and
    serve.

Selections per serving:
    1 Bread
    1½ Fat
    ¼ Fruit
    1 Protein
    ¼ Vegetable
    5 Optional Calories

Orange Sunrise

Serves 2
155 Calories per serving

Adapt this recipe to suit your own taste, for example replace the orange juice and sultanas with grape juice and chopped dried peaches.

1oz (30g) flaked rice

½ pint (300ml) orange juice

1oz (30g) sultanas

1 teaspoon sugar or honey

Selections per serving:
  ½ Bread
  1½ Fruit
  20 Optional Calories

1 Place the rice into a dish or deep bowl. Stir the orange juice and sultanas into the dish then cover and cook on HIGH for 4 minutes, stir well then cover and cook on HIGH for a further 6 minutes, stirring every 2 minutes.

2 Remove the thickened dessert from the oven and leave to stand for 1 minute. Stir the sugar or honey into the dessert and divide between two ramekins or small dishes. Serve hot or chilled.

Fruity Tapioca Pudding

Serves 4
155 Calories per serving

The dried fruits sweeten this pudding but if you wish add artificial sweetener.

1½ pints (900ml) skimmed milk

2oz (60g) mixture of dried fruit, ready-to-eat dried apricots, peaches, prunes, raisins and sultanas

finely grated zest of ¼-½ lemon

2oz (60g) tapioca

Selections per serving:
  ½ Bread
  ½ Fruit
  ¾ Milk

1 Pour the milk into a large bowl.

2 Chop the fruit into small pieces then stir into the milk. Add the lemon zest and tapioca, stir well.

3 Place the bowl, uncovered, in the oven and cook on HIGH for 8 minutes.

4 Stir the mixture well then continue cooking on MEDIUM for 8 minutes stirring every 2 minutes. Leave to stand for 6 minutes, stir well and serve.

Spiced Sago Pudding

Serves 4
175 Calories per serving

Keep the sago and milk well covered during cooking or the liquid will evaporate and the pudding will become very thick.

1½ pints (900ml) skimmed milk

3oz (90g) sago

1½ tablespoons sugar

1 teaspoon cinnamon

Selections per serving:
  ¾ Bread
  ¾ Milk
  25 Optional Calories

1   Pour the milk into a large bowl, stir in the sago and sugar.

2   Cover the bowl with pierced clingfilm then transfer to the microwave and cook on HIGH for 8 minutes.

3   Carefully turn back just under a quarter of the clingfilm, just enough to be able to stir the pudding. Add the cinnamon and stir well.

4   Return the pudding to the oven and cook on MEDIUM for 7 minutes, stirring every 2 minutes. Leave to stand for 5 minutes before serving.

Sweet Couscous

Serves 4
280 Calories per serving

This is a favourite recipe of mine. If you haven't eaten couscous before try this dish and then experiment adding it to sweet and savoury recipes.

2oz (60g) dried dates

2oz (60g) dried ready-to-eat peaches or apricots

1oz (30g) raisins

4fl oz (120ml) pineapple juice

6oz (180g) couscous

5fl oz (150ml) low-fat natural yogurt

Selections per serving:
  1½ Bread
  1½ Fruit
  ¼ Milk

1 Place the dried dates, peaches and raisins on a chopping board and roughly chop all the fruit.

2 Transfer the fruit to a bowl, pour over the pineapple juice and leave to soak for 1-2 hours.

3 Place the couscous in a container, stir in ¼ pint (150ml) cold water and the soaked fruits and their liquid, cover and cook on HIGH for 3 minutes. Fluff up the grains of couscous and leave to stand for 4-5 minutes.

4 Fluff the couscous and fruit up once again, cover and leave to cool.

5 Divide the Sweet Couscous between four serving dishes, make a deep hole in the centre of each dish and spoon the yogurt into the hole. Serve within 2 hours or the couscous will soak up the yogurt and the grains will no longer be separate.

Ground Rice Pudding

Serves 2
230 Calories per serving

To cut down on calories the maple syrup may be substituted with artificial sweetener and 45 Calories deducted from each serving.

1 pint (600ml) skimmed milk

1½oz (45g) ground rice

finely grated zest of ½ a lemon

finely grated zest of ½ an orange

1½ tablespoons maple syrup

Selections per serving:
  ¾ Bread
  1 Milk
  45 Optional Calories

1   Pour the milk into a container or bowl. Stir in the rice, lemon and orange zests.

2   Place the ground rice mixture in the oven and cook, uncovered, on HIGH for 5 minutes, stir well.

3   Return the rice mixture to the oven and cook on HIGH, uncovered, for a further 3 minutes, stirring every minute. Leave to stand for 2 minutes.

4   Stir the maple syrup into the cooked rice and serve.

Thick Rice Pudding

Serves 4
100 Calories per serving

This pudding can be served hot or cold. It thickens on cooling so use the cold rice pudding to make a fruit condé, or spoon on top of hot stewed fruit.

2oz (60g) short grain rice

1 pint (600ml) skimmed milk

1 tablespoon sugar

Selections per serving:
  ½ Bread
  ½ Milk
  15 Optional Calories

1   Place the rice in a large bowl, stir in the milk and sugar. Cover the bowl with a piece of clingfilm then pull back to leave about a quarter uncovered.

2   Cook on HIGH for 6 minutes until boiling. Stir well. Reduce the power to LOW and cook for 35 minutes, stirring about every 10 minutes. Leave to stand for 5 minutes.

Semolina Flan

Serves 8
165 Calories per serving

Make the semolina base in advance but complete the recipe a short time before it is to be served or the marmalade glaze and fruit juices may start to run.

1 pint (600ml) skimmed milk

finely grated zest of 1 lemon

4oz (120g) semolina

2 eggs, lightly beaten

5 tablespoons sieved marmalade

12 medium greengages

1 Pour the milk into a large bowl, add the lemon zest and cook, uncovered, on HIGH for 6 minutes until boiling. Sprinkle the semolina into the milk and stir well.

2 Cook, uncovered, on HIGH for 2 minutes 30 seconds, stirring once or twice during the cooking time until very thick. Leave for 1 minute 30 seconds.

3 Stir in the eggs, mix well and cook on MEDIUM for 1 minute 30 seconds, stirring every 30 seconds. Remove from the heat and stir 3 tablespoons marmalade into the thick mixture.

4 Line a dish about 9 × 6 inches (22.5 × 15 cm) with non-stick baking parchment. Spoon the thick semolina into the dish and level the surface. Leave until cold, then chill for 1-2 hours until firm.

5 Place a chopping board or large flat plate over the dish and invert onto the board. Remove the baking parchment.

6 Halve the greengages then cut into thin wedges and arrange in lines along the semolina base.

7 Spoon the remaining marmalade into a cup or small bowl and heat on HIGH for 40-50 seconds until warm and very slightly runny. Brush the marmalade over the greengage wedges, leave until the marmalade is cool then cut into eight pieces and serve.

Selections per serving:
  ½ Bread
  ¾ Fruit
  ¼ Milk
  ¼ Protein
  30 Optional Calories

Porridge

Serves 1
115 Calories per serving

The following recipes are for Porridge made with quick porridge oats or the traditional recipe made with oatmeal. The amount of liquid will vary according to the size of container in which it is cooked and to personal preferences. During cooking allow plenty of room for the mixture to rise, and stir to prevent the oats or oatmeal sticking in lumps. Cover after the cooking time with a plate or lid as cooking continues for 1-2 minutes after the power is switched off.

1oz (30g) porridge oats

7fl oz (210ml) water

Selections per serving:
  1 Bread

1   Place the porridge oats in a bowl, add the water, stir around.

2   Place in the oven and cook, uncovered, for 3 minutes stirring every minute. Cover and leave to stand for 1-2 minutes.

Traditional Porridge

Serves 1
115 Calories per serving

1oz (30g) medium oatmeal

scant 9fl oz (270ml) water

Selections per serving:
  1 Bread

1   Place the oatmeal and water in a bowl, stir round.

2   Place in the oven and cook, uncovered, for 5 minutes 30 seconds, stirring three or four times during the cooking time.

3   Cover and leave to stand for 1-2 minutes.

Vegetables

Vegetables cook extremely well in the microwave oven. Only a little water is required, and sometimes none at all. They retain a great deal of their colour, flavour, texture and nutritional content.

Buy vegetables which are really fresh, high-quality and in good condition. When particular vegetables are in season, their quality good and price reasonable, it may be worth buying some for home freezing. As little water is necessary and cooking is quick it is possible to blanch small amounts of vegetables very successfully in the microwave.

Frozen vegetables require little or no additional water for cooking, just place in a suitable container so they form a single layer, cover and cook on HIGH for the recommended time. As with all foods the structure of the vegetable, its density, starting temperature and shape affect the time and evenness of cooking. Whenever possible cut vegetables into even-sized pieces so they cook evenly. Arrange vegetables such as cauliflower and asparagus, which have florets or delicate tips, with the delicate, less dense ends towards the centre of the container. A whole head of cauliflower is not particularly well suited to microwaving but by turning it upside down halfway through the cooking time the texture should not be altered greatly.

The quantity and weight of the vegetables drastically alters cooking times. For example one 6oz (180g) potato would only take about 4 minutes to cook but four potatoes would take about 12 minutes. If you wanted to serve a large number at a party it would be advisable to cook them in a conventional oven. As a general rule cooking vegetables for up to four people saves a considerable amount of time and is economical. Some vegetables, for example beetroot, are cooked in a far shorter time than normal. Two small beetroot can be cooked in under 10 minutes by microwaving whereas normally it takes about an hour and the smell spreads from the kitchen into other rooms.

The chart opposite should be used as a guide for the preparation and cooking of vegetables. The preparation is usually very similar to conventionally cooked vegetables but it is important to remember that all food encased in a skin must be pierced several times to prevent them bursting and exploding over the oven. Never add salt. Unless otherwise stated, cover the containers with a lid which allows some of the steam to escape, or cover loosely with clingfilm, pull the film over the container but leave a small gap at one side and do not allow the film to touch the vegetables. I advise stirring vegetables during cooking, it is not always essential but ensures more even cooking. Leave the vegetables to stand in their container for about 2 mintues, this completes the cooking process.

Cooking Guidelines for Vegetables

Vegetable & Weight	Setting	Time	Additional instructions
artichoke, globe 2	HIGH	8 mins	Cut off the stalks, cut about 1 inch (2.5cm) from the tops and trim the spiny tips from the leaves. Open the inner leaves and scoop out the 'hairy' choke. Add 6 tablespoons water.
asparagus 8oz (240g)	HIGH	4 mins	Scrape off the outer scales, arrange in a circle with the tips towards the centre and slightly overlapping. Add 2 tablespoons water.
aubergine 8oz (240g)	HIGH	5 mins	Cut in thick slices or cubes, sprinkle with salt and leave in a sieve for 30 minutes, rinse well under running cold water. Add 4 tablespoons water. Stir once during cooking.
beans, broad 8oz (240g)	HIGH	4½ mins	Shell. Add 4 tablespoons water, stir once during cooking.
beans, thin or Kenyan 8oz (240g)	HIGH	5 mins	Top and tail. Add 4 tablespoons water, stir once during cooking.
beans, dwarf 8oz (240g)	HIGH	7½ mins	Top and tail. Add 4 tablespoons water, stir once during cooking.
beans, runner 8oz (240g)	HIGH	4½ mins	Cook very young beans as dwarf, top and tail others then remove the strings from the sides and cut into ½ inch (1.25cm) diagonal slices. Stir once during cooking.
beetroot 2 × 4oz (120g)	HIGH	8½ mins	Leave whole, do not peel. Add 5 tablespoons water, turn 180 degrees halfway through cooking.
broccoli calabrese 8oz (240g)	HIGH	5 mins	Divide into even-sized florets, arrange with the heads towards the centre. Add 3 tablespoons water.
Brussels sprouts 8oz (240g)	HIGH	4 mins	Remove any discoloured leaves, cut a cross in the stalk. Add 2 tablespoons water, stir once during cooking.
cabbage 8oz (240g)	HIGH	5 mins	Remove any discoloured leaves, shred. Add 2 tablespoons water, stir once during cooking.
carrot, whole 8oz (240g)	HIGH	5 mins	Choose small even-sized young carrots, add 2 tablespoons water, stir once during cooking.
carrot, sliced/sticks 8oz (240g)	HIGH	5 mins	Cut into thin slices or 1½ inch (4cm) sticks, add 2 tablespoons water. Stir once during cooking.
cauliflower 8oz (240g)	HIGH	4½ mins	Divide into even-sized florets with heads towards the centre. Add 3 tablespoons water.
celeriac 8oz (240g)	HIGH	6 mins	Cut into ¾ inch (2cm) or 1×1½ inch (2.5×4cm) sticks. Add ½ teaspoon lemon juice and 2 tablespoons water. Stir once during cooking.
celery 8oz (240g)	HIGH	6 mins	Cut into 2 inch (5cm) lengths. Add 2 tablespoons water. Stir once during cooking.

Vegetable & Weight	Setting	Time	Additional instructions
corn on cob, baby 6oz (180g) whole	HIGH	4 mins	Add 2 tablespoons water.
1 corn on the cob, 8oz (240g)	HIGH	4 mins	Remove leaves and silky threads. Wrap in lightly greased greaseproof paper. Turn halfway through cooking time.
2 corn on the cobs, 8oz (240g)	HIGH	7 mins	
courgette 8oz (240g)	HIGH	3 mins	Cut into thick slices or quarter lengthways then cut into 1½ inch (4cm) lengths. Do not add water, stir once during cooking.
fennel 8oz (240g)	HIGH	5½ mins	Cut in thick slices or quarter small bulbs. Add 3 tablespoons water. Stir once during cooking.
leeks, baby 8oz (240g)	HIGH	6 mins	Halve, add 2 tablespoons water, stir once during cooking.
leeks, common 8oz (240g)	HIGH	4 mins	Cut into 1 inch (2.5cm) thick slices. Add 2 tablespoons water, stir once during cooking.
marrow 8oz (240g)	HIGH	3 mins	Peel, seed and cut into 1 inch (2.5cm) thick slices. Do not add water. Rearrange halfway through cooking time.
mushrooms 8oz (240g)	HIGH	2 mins	Leave small button mushrooms whole, halve or slice others. Do not add water, stir once during cooking.
onions, small whole 8oz (240g)	HIGH	3½ mins	Add 2 tablespoons water. Stir once during cooking.
onions, sliced 8oz (240g)	HIGH	3½ mins	Add 2 tablespoons water, Stir once during cooking.
parsnips 8oz (240g)	HIGH	3 mins	Peel, cut in chunks or thick slices. Add 3 tablespoons water, stir once during cooking.
peas, garden 8oz (240g)	HIGH	5 mins	Shell. Add 2 tablespoons water, stir once during cooking.
peas, mangetout 8oz (240g)	HIGH	3 mins	Top and tail. Add 2 tablespoons water, stir once during cooking.
peas, sugar 8oz (240g)	HIGH	3½ mins	Top and tail. Add 2 tablespoons water, stir once during cooking.
potatoes, new 6oz (180g)	HIGH	4½ mins	Scrape, leave small whole, thickly slice others. Add 3 tablespoons water. Stir once during cooking.
potatoes, old 6oz (180g)	HIGH	5 mins	Peel, cut in 1½ inch (4cm) chunks. Add 3 tablespoons water. Stir once during cooking.
potatoes, whole baked			Prick all over, place on kitchen paper.
1 × 6oz (180g)	HIGH	4½ mins	
2 × 6oz (180g)	HIGH	7½ mins	
spinach 8oz (240g)	HIGH	3½ mins	Wash well then shake to remove excess water. Do not add water. Stir during cooking.
swede 8oz (240g)	HIGH	5 mins	Peel, cut into ¾ inch (2cm) cubes. Add 2 tablespoons water. Stir once during cooking.
turnips 8oz (240g)	HIGH	4 mins	Peel, halve the very tiny baby turnips, cut the others into ¾ inch (4cm) cubes. Add 2 tablespoons water. Stir once during cooking.

Cabbage in Orange Sauce

Serves 4
60 Calories per serving

The sharp flavour of the orange and the sweetness of the sugar gives the cabbage a sweet and sour flavour. If you like add a little soy sauce to the completed dish.

12oz (360g) white cabbage

2 medium oranges

¼-½ teaspoon fennel seeds

2 teaspoons cornflour

3 tablespoons water

1 teaspoon sugar

Selections per serving:
½ Fruit
1 Vegetable
10 Optional Calories

1   Finely shred the cabbage, place in a container.

2   Using a zester remove the zest from half an orange – alternatively use a potato peeler to remove the orange zest and then cut into very fine strips. Squeeze the juice from the oranges.

3   Stir the orange juice and fennel seeds together with the cabbage, cover and cook on HIGH for 6 minutes.

4   Blend the cornflour to a smooth paste with the water, add the sugar then stir into the hot cabbage. Cover the dish and continue cooking on MEDIUM for 5 minutes, stirring occasionally. Leave to stand for 2 minutes. Serve hot or cold.

Mangetout Salad

Serves 2
130 Calories per serving

Microwaving can be a convenient way to brown nuts but ovens vary considerably. I have used one oven which took 10 minutes to brown 2oz (60g) desiccated coconut, yet another took only 2 minutes 30 seconds. If your oven takes a long time, brown all nuts under a hot grill.

8oz (240g) mangetout

½oz (15g) flaked almonds

¼ inch (5mm) slice ginger, finely chopped

1½ teaspoons sesame oil

½ teaspoon lemon juice

Selections per serving:
  1 Fat
  ½ Protein
  1½ Vegetable

1 Top and tail the mangetout. Place in a container, add 2 tablespoons water then cover and cook on HIGH for 2 minutes. Stir once during cooking. Drain and place in a bowl.

2 Spread the flaked almonds evenly over a plate. Cook on HIGH, start checking to see how quickly the almonds are browning after 1 minute, stir every 40-50 seconds, until very light brown.

3 In a cup or small bowl mix the ginger, sesame oil and lemon juice together until completely combined.

4 Pour the ginger dressing over the mangetout, stir well then add the flaked almonds. Serve hot or chilled.

Vegetable Mix

Serves 6
145 Calories per serving

This dish is similar to a hot coleslaw. It can be served as an accompaniment to a variety of main dishes.

6oz (180g) white cabbage

6oz (180g) parsnip

1 medium onion

3 carrots

15oz (440g) can chopped tomatoes

1 teaspoon chilli sauce

salt

Selections per serving:
  ¼ Bread
  1½ Vegetable
  5 Optional Calories

1 Finely shred or grate the cabbage, parsnip, onion and carrots.

2 Place the tomatoes in a bowl or suitable container, stir in the chilli sauce and prepared vegetables and mix well – the mixture will be very thick.

3 Cover the mixture and cook on HIGH for 8 minutes, stirring two or three times during cooking. Stand for 4 minutes. Season with a little salt and serve.

VARIATION
Add 1½oz (45g) roughly chopped peanuts to the prepared vegetables.

Selections per serving:
  ¼ Bread
  ¼ Fat
  ½ Protein
  1½ Vegetable
  5 Optional Calories
  185 Calories per serving for this variation

Aubergine Dip

Serves 4
120 Calories per serving

This quick and simple dip should be served in very small ramekins and surrounded with crudités. It makes an unusual starter suitable for a luncheon or dinner party.

---

1 medium aubergine, 10-11oz (300-330g)

4 tablespoons cream cheese

2oz (60g) curd cheese

1 small clove garlic, crushed

1-2 teaspoons lemon juice

salt and pepper

12oz (360g) mixture of carrots, celery, cucumber and cauliflower florets

Selections per serving:
¼ Protein
1¾ Vegetable
100 Optional Calories

1 Prick the aubergine all over with a fork, place on a plate and cook, uncovered, on HIGH for 4 minutes 30 seconds. Leave until cool enough to handle.

2 Cut the aubergine in half and scoop out all the flesh.

3 Place the aubergine, cream and curd cheeses in a liquidiser and process to a purée.

4 Transfer the aubergine purée to a bowl, add the crushed garlic and lemon juice and season to taste with salt and pepper.

5 If the dip is to be served warm leave in the bowl otherwise spoon into four small ramekins.

6 Cut the carrots, celery and cucumber into small 1½ inch (4cm) long sticks, divide the cauliflower into very small florets. Arrange the crudités on four serving plates around the ramekins.

7 If the dip is to be served warm cover the bowl and cook on HIGH for 1 minute 30 seconds, stir well then spoon into the ramekin dishes.

Stuffed Onions

Serves 4
100 Calories per serving

The large Spanish onions are ideal for this recipe, they have a pleasant mild flavour.

---

4 large onions, approximately 2-2¼lb (1-1.1kg)

1½oz (45g) breadcrumbs

½oz (15g) Parmesan cheese, finely grated

½ teaspoon sage

pepper sauce

Selections per serving:
¼ Bread
3 Vegetable
20 Optional Calories

1   Peel the onions and cut a thin slice from the top and base of each one.

2   Using a sharp knife and a grapefruit knife gradually remove the centre of the onion leaving only two or three layers. Finely chop the onion slices and the centres.

3   Place the chopped onions in a dish without any water, cover and cook on HIGH for 5 minutes.

4   Mix the breadcrumbs, cheese and sage with the hot onion and season generously with two or three dashes of pepper sauce.

5   Spoon the stuffing into the onions – do not pack too firmly. Then arrange in a circle in a dish, add 3 tablespoons water and cook on HIGH for 6 minutes, turning the onions 90 degrees twice during the cooking time. Leave to stand for 3 minutes.

Chinese-Style Vegetables

Serves 4
190 Calories per serving

This recipe should be used as a guide. Look at the cooking chart on pages 145-146 and substitute the same weight of a vegetable which has the cooking time as one already in the recipe, add it in the same sequence and the crisp texture of all the vegetables should remain.

3oz (90g) carrot

1oz (30g) mouli (white radish)

3oz (90g) courgette

3oz (90g) cauliflower florets

½ onion

½ red pepper

1oz (30g) medium-size button mushrooms

2oz (60g) mangetout

1 tablespoon sesame oil

3oz (90g) beansprouts

1½ tablespoons soy sauce

1 tablespoon sesame seeds

Selections per serving:
¾ Fat
1½ Vegetable
15 Optional Calories

1   Cut the carrot, mouli and courgette into 1½ inch (4cm) lengths about ½ inch (1.25cm) wide.

2   Divide the cauliflower into very small florets.

3   Slice the onion and red pepper to make half rings.

4   Halve the mushrooms and top and tail the mangetout.

5   Place the oil, onion, carrot, mouli and cauliflower in a bowl, add 2 tablespoons water and stir round.

6   Partially cover the bowl with clingfilm or lid. Cook on HIGH for 3 minutes.

7   Add the courgette and red pepper, stir round then cover and cook on HIGH for 2 minutes.

8   Add the mushrooms, mangetout, beansprouts and soy sauce, stir round then cover and cook on HIGH for 1 minute 30 seconds.

9   Stir in the sesame seeds and leave to stand for 2 minutes.

Stuffed Tomatoes

Serves 4
140 Calories per serving

The large marmande or beefsteak tomatoes are well worth filling as they hold a large amount of filling and retain their shape well.

4 large marmande tomatoes

1 clove garlic

1 medium onion

1 teaspoon oil

4oz (120g) wholemeal breadcrumbs

2oz (60g) lean cooked ham, diced

1 tablespoon chopped parsley

1 teaspoon marjoram

Selections per serving:
  1 Bread
  ¼ Fat
  ½ Protein
  2 Vegetable

1 Cut a thin slice from the top of each tomato and set aside.

2 Scoop out all the flesh and seeds from the tomatoes. Discard the seeds and chop the flesh.

3 Finely chop the garlic and onion, then place in a container with the oil, cover and cook on HIGH for 4 minutes until the onions are soft.

4 Mix the breadcrumbs, ham and herbs into the onion mixture.

5 Spoon the stuffing into the tomato shells, gently press the stuffing into the tomato. Lay the tomato slices on top and place in a suitable dish.

6 Cover the dish and cook on HIGH for 4 minutes 30 seconds, leave to stand for 2 minutes then serve.

Stuffed Aubergines

Serves 2
165 Calories per serving

I am particularly fond of this recipe as the aubergines retain their texture and the smoky flavour of the cheese is delicious.

---

1 small aubergine, about 12oz (360g)

salt

1 onion

1 tomato

½ clove garlic, crushed

2 teaspoons tomato purée

2oz (60g) smoked cheese, grated

Selections per serving:
1 Protein
3 Vegetable
5 Optional Calories

1   Cut the aubergine in half along its length. Make three or four deep cuts from the cut side towards, but not through, the skin, then sprinkle liberally with salt. Lay the halves in a colander and leave for about 30 minutes to allow the bitter juices to drip away. Rinse very well under running cold water.

2   Using a grapefruit knife scoop out the inside of each aubergine half, leaving a shell of about ½ inch (1.25cm). Roughly chop the scooped out aubergine.

3   Lay the aubergine cut-side down in a container, add 3 tablespoons water, cover and cook on HIGH for 3 minutes. Turn each half upside down, cover and cook on HIGH for a further 2 minutes.

4   Finely chop the onion and roughly chop the tomato. Place the onion, tomato, chopped aubergine, garlic and tomato purée in a container, cover and cook on HIGH for 3 minutes 30 seconds.

5   Stir the smoked cheese into the onion and tomato mixture then spoon into the hot aubergine shells. Lay the halves in a container and cook uncovered for 1 minute.

Leeks with Grapefruit

Serves 4
35 Calories per serving

If you are unable to buy baby leeks substitute young thin leeks and cut into ½ inch (1.25cm) slices.

9oz (270g) baby leeks

1 medium grapefruit

1 teaspoon cornflour

1. Cut the leeks in half and place in a container which will hold the leeks in a single layer.

2. Cut the grapefruit in half lengthways. Squeeze the juice from one half and add 2 tablespoons of the juice to the leeks.

3. Cover the container and cook on HIGH for 6 minutes. Leave to stand for 2 minutes.

4. Blend the cornflour with the remaining grapefruit juice.

5. Drain the leeks, reserve the cooking liquid and stir into the cornflour paste. Return the leeks to the container and add the grapefruit sauce. Cover the container and cook on HIGH for 1 minute, stirring every 20-30 seconds.

6. Using a sharp knife cut the peel and all the pith from the remaining grapefruit, divide into segments and cut each segment in half. Add the grapefruit segments to the leeks directly they are removed from the oven, leave to stand for 2 minutes.

Selections per serving:
½ Fruit
¾ Vegetable
5 Optional Calories

Stuffed Mushrooms

Serves 2
250 Calories per serving

Mushrooms must never be overcooked or they lose their texture and eventually collapse. If in doubt about the cooking time remove the mushrooms from the oven, allow to stand and then, if necessary, return to the oven for a few more seconds.

2 × 3oz (90g) large cap or flat mushrooms

1 tablespoon sesame oil

2 tablespoons finely chopped spring onions

½ red pepper

2oz (60g) smoked cheese or mature Cheddar cheese

1oz (30g) breadcrumbs

salt and pepper

Selections per serving:
  ½ Bread
  1½ Fat
  1 Protein
  1 Vegetable

1 Remove the stalks from the mushrooms and chop finely.

2 Brush all over the mushroom caps with sesame oil. Place the remaining oil in a bowl and add the spring onions.

3 Finely chop the red pepper and add to the spring onions, cover and cook on HIGH for 1 minute 30 seconds.

4 Stir the chopped mushrooms into the bowl, cover and cook on HIGH for 1 minute 30 seconds.

5 Finely grate the cheese and then stir into the spring onion mixture. Mix in the breadcrumbs and season with salt and pepper.

6 Spoon the breadcrumb mixture evenly over the mushrooms and transfer to a shallow dish. Cover and cook on HIGH for 1 minute 30 seconds. Do not overcook or the mushrooms will ooze out their moisture. Leave to stand for 3 minutes.

Stuffed Marrow

Serves 4
115 Calories per serving

Marrows contain a high proportion of water so do not add any when cooking them in a microwave or they will lose their texture.

---

1 medium marrow, approx 2¼lb (1.1kg)

1 medium onion

4 teaspoons flour

8oz (240g) can chopped tomatoes

½ teaspoon fennel seeds

½ teaspoon basil

4oz (120g) mushrooms, chopped

6oz (180g) smoked tofu, grated

salt and pepper

Selections per serving:
   ¾ Protein
   3 Vegetable
   10 Optional Calories

1   Peel the marrow then cut in half along its length and scoop out all the seeds.

2   Lay the halves in a dish, cover and cook on HIGH for 5 minutes. Turn the marrow halves 180 degrees so the sides nearest to the centre of the dish turn to the outer edge. Leave the marrow to stand while making the stuffing.

3   Finely chop the onion, place in a container without additional water, cover and cook on HIGH for 3 minutes.

4   Stir the flour into the onion then stir in the tomatoes, fennel seeds, basil, mushrooms and tofu. Season with a little salt and pepper. Cover and cook on HIGH for 5 minutes, stirring once during the cooking time.

5   Spoon the tomato and tofu stuffing into the marrow halves, cover and cook on HIGH for 1 minute 30 seconds, leave to stand for 2 minutes.

Braised Celery

Serves 2
10 Calories per serving

This is a very simple quick recipe, it may be served with a hot or cold meal.

8oz (240g) celery

¼ pint (150ml) boiling stock

1 Cut the celery into 3 inch (7.5cm) lengths, cut the thinner ends of the sticks a little larger. Place the celery into a suitable container and pour over the boiling stock.

2 Cover the container with a lid or piece of clingfilm and turn back a little of the clingfilm, large enough to stir the celery.

Selections per serving:
   1½ Vegetable

3 Cook the celery on HIGH for 6-7 minutes, stirring halfway through the cooking time.

French-Style Peas

Serves 4
75 Calories per serving

2 teaspoons margarine

4 tablespoons finely chopped spring onions

12oz (360g) frozen petit pois

1½ teaspoons mint jelly

2 or 3 lettuce leaves

salt and pepper

Selections per serving:
   ¾ Bread
   ½ Fat
   5 Optional Calories

1 Place the margarine and spring onions in a container, cover and cook on HIGH for 1 minute.

2 Stir the petit pois and mint jelly into the spring onions, cover and cook on HIGH for 2 minutes, stir well then cook on HIGH for a further 2 minutes.

3 Finely shred the lettuce and stir into the peas. Cook on HIGH for 1 minute. Leave to stand for 2 minutes then season with salt and pepper and serve.

Peperonata

Serves 4
100 Calories per serving

If yellow peppers are very expensive or poor quality replace with an extra green or red pepper.

1 clove garlic

1 onion

1 large red pepper

1 large green pepper

1 large yellow pepper

1 tablespoon olive oil

1lb (480g) tomatoes

10 small black olives

salt and pepper

Selections per serving:
  1 Fat
  1½ Vegetable

1   Finely chop the garlic. Cut the onion in half then cut thinly to form half slices.

2   Remove the cores and seeds from the peppers, cut in thin strips.

3   Place the oil, garlic, onions and peppers in a container, cover and cook on HIGH for 5 minutes.

4   Roughly chop the tomatoes. Halve then stone the olives.

5   Stir the tomatoes and olives into the pepper mixture.

6   Cover and cook on HIGH for 8 minutes, stirring twice during the cooking time.

7   Remove the lid from the Peperonata and continue cooking on HIGH for 4 minutes, stirring occasionally. Leave to stand for 4 minutes. Season with salt and pepper.

Jacket Potatoes

Serves 1
155 Calories per serving

1×6oz (180g) potato

Scrub the potato and prick well. Place on a double thickness of kitchen paper and cook on HIGH for 4 minutes 30 seconds. Leave to stand 3 minutes. Serve alone or with one of the toppings or fillings below.

Selections per serving:
2 Bread

For two servings cook 2× 6oz (180g) potatoes on HIGH for 8 minutes.

VARIATIONS
Soured Cream Topping
Mix 1½ tablespoons soured cream together with 2 teaspoons chopped chives.
Add 75 Optional Calories

Yogurt Topping
2 tablespoons low-fat natural yogurt mixed together with 2 teaspoons chopped chives.
Add 20 Optional Calories per serving

FILLING 1
235 Calories per serving

1×6 oz (180g) hot jacket potato

3oz (90g) baked beans in tomato sauce

2 teaspoons finely grated Parmesan cheese

1　Prepare and cook the potato as described, keep warm.

2　Spoon the beans in tomato sauce into a container, cover and heat on HIGH for 1 minute 10 seconds.

3　Split the potato in half, spoon the baked beans on top of the potato and sprinkle with the Parmesan cheese. Leave to stand for 2 minutes. If the cheese has not melted during the standing time return to the oven for a few seconds.

To serve two, double all the quantities, reheat the beans on HIGH for 2 minutes.

Selections per serving:
　2 Bread
　1 Protein
　20 Optional Calories

FILLING 2
350 Calories per serving

1×6oz (180g) hot jacket potato

½ onion, finely chopped

1 × 1¼oz (40g) frankfurter

2 teaspoons skimmed milk

½ teaspoon mustard

½oz (15g) cheese, grated

1   Prepare and cook the potato as described, keep warm.

2   Place the onion in a container, without any water, cover and cook on HIGH for 2 minutes.

3   Place the frankfurter on a microwave rack and cook on HIGH for 30 seconds.

4   Cut the potato in half, scoop out all the flesh leaving the skins intact.

5   Mash the potato with the milk, add the onion and mustard and mix again. Chop the frankfurter and add to the mixture together with the grated cheese.

6   Spoon the stuffing back into the potato skins, place on a plate and cook, uncovered, on HIGH for 50-60 seconds.

   To serve two, double all the quantities but cook the onion for 3 minutes and the frankfurters for 40 seconds. Reheat on HIGH for 1 minute 30 seconds.

Selections per serving:
   2 Bread
   1½ Protein
   ½ Vegetable
   5 Optional Calories

FILLING 3
270 Calories per serving

1×6oz (180g) hot jacket potato

½oz (15g) Danish Blue or blue soft cheese, eg Blue Brie

2oz (60g) cottage cheese

1 teaspoon skimmed milk

¼ teaspoon mustard

1   Prepare and cook the potato as described, keep warm.

2   Cut the potato in half, scoop out all the flesh leaving the skins intact.

3   Crumble or cut the blue cheese into small pieces. Mash the potato together with the blue cheese, cottage cheese, milk and mustard.

4   Spoon the filling back into the potato skins, lay on a plate and cook, uncovered, on HIGH for 50-60 seconds.

   To serve two people, double all the ingredients and reheat on HIGH for 1 minute 30 seconds.

Selections per serving:
   2 Bread
   1½ Protein
   5 Optional Calories

Ratatouille

Serves 4
135 Calories per serving

This well-known dish can be made in the microwave but take care not to overcook the vegetables or they will be mushy. They should keep their shape and colour.

1 large aubergine

salt

2 cloves garlic

1 onion

2 teaspoons olive oil

1 green pepper

1 red pepper

2 courgettes

1½ teaspoons tomato purée

1lb (480g) tomatoes, chopped

pepper
Selections per serving:
  ½ Fat
  3½ Vegetable
  5 Optional Calories

1 Cut the aubergine into chunks, about 1½ inches (4cm) in size. Place in a sieve and sprinkle liberally with salt. Leave for 30-40 minutes to allow the bitter juices to drip away. Rinse well under running cold water.

2 Finely chop the garlic and onion.

3 Place the olive oil, garlic and onion in a bowl, cover and cook on HIGH for 2 minutes.

4 Core and remove the seeds from the peppers, cut into 1 inch (2.5cm) squares.

5 Thickly slice the courgettes.

6 Add the peppers to the onions, cover and cook on HIGH for 3 minutes.

7 Stir the tomato purée, chopped tomatoes, courgettes and aubergine into the onion mixture, cover and cook on HIGH for 8 minutes. Stir once during cooking. Leave to stand for 4 minutes. Season with salt and pepper.

Creamed Onions

Serves 4
105 Calories per serving
This recipe makes an unusual vegetable accompaniment.

2 large onions (approximately 14oz/420g)

1 tablespoon margarine

12fl oz (360ml) skimmed milk

1oz (30g) cornflour

salt and pepper

Selections per serving:
¼ Bread
¾ Fat
¼ Milk
1¼ Vegetable
5 Optional Calories

1 Thinly slice the onions.

2 Place the margarine in a container, melt on HIGH for about 50 seconds.

3 Add the onions, stir then cover and cook on HIGH for 7 minutes, stirring every 2 minutes. Leave to stand while preparing the sauce.

4 Blend the milk together with the cornflour, place in the oven and cook uncovered on HIGH for 4 minutes, stirring every 40-50 seconds until thick and boiling.

5 Stir the sauce into the onions and return to the oven for 30 seconds, stir well and leave to stand for 2 minutes. Season with salt and pepper.

Acorn Squash Purée

Serves 4
140 Calories per serving

More and more unusual and exotic fruits and vegetables are being grown in this country and imported all the time. When I first saw an acorn squash in a supermarket I didn't know how to cook it so took one home to experiment. This is the very simple purée I made.

1 medium acorn squash (approximately 2¼lb/1.1kg)

3 tablespoons single cream

nutmeg, grated

salt and pepper

1 Cut the squash in half — it will be extremely hard so use a very sharp knife.

2 Scoop out all the seeds and lay cut side down on a flat plate.

3 Cook on HIGH for 10 minutes, turning the squash 180 degrees during the cooking time but do not turn over, the cut side should remain flat against the plate.

4 Leave the squash on the plate to cool.

5 Using a spoon scoop all the flesh out of the squash skins. Transfer the flesh to a bowl and mash well until smooth. Beat the cream and some freshly grated nutmeg into the purée. Season well with salt and pepper.

6 Cover the purée and reheat on HIGH for 3-5 minutes, stirring every 1 minute 30 seconds. The time for reheating will depend on the starting temperature of the purée.

Selections per serving:
 1¾ Vegetable
 35 Optional Calories

Spicy Mushrooms

Serves 4
55 Calories per serving

These mushrooms make an appetising starter served with thin slices of melba toast but remember to add the additional Selections or calories.

1 clove garlic

2 tablespoons grated or finely chopped onion

2½ tablespoons stock or water

¼ teaspoon ground cinnamon

¼ teaspoon ground coriander

12oz (360g) small button mushrooms

2 teaspoons cornflour

4 tablespoons soured cream

salt and pepper

1 teaspoon chopped coriander

Selections per serving:
  1 Vegetable
  55 Optional Calories

1 Finely chop the garlic then place in a container with the onion and 1½ tablespoons stock or water. Add the ground spices, stir round then cover and cook on HIGH for 1 minute 30 seconds.

2 Thinly slice the mushrooms.

3 Stir the mushrooms into the onion mixture then cover and cook on HIGH for 2 minutes.

4 Blend the cornflour to a smooth paste with the remaining stock or water.

5 Stir the cornflour paste into the hot mushrooms, return to the oven and cook, uncovered, on HIGH for 1 minute. Stir once or twice during the cooking time.

6 Leave the mushrooms to stand for 3 minutes, stir in the soured cream and season well with salt and pepper.

7 Spoon the mushrooms and the sauce into four small ramekins, sprinkle with the chopped coriander and serve.

Fruit

Microwaved fruits will retain their shape and have a good texture, colour and flavour if a few basic principles are followed. The fruit should always be high quality and prepared and cooked as soon after purchase or picking as possible. The exception to the rule is when fruit is cooked to make jam. A microwave doesn't enable the fruit to cook slowly enough. This is essential for most jams because pectin, the setting agent naturally present in fruits, requires long slow cooking if it is to be extracted. It is possible to make small quantities of some jams and marmalades, and recipes for Strawberry Jam and Three Fruit Marmalade are included in this section.

All fruit encased in a skin must be pierced before cooking or the fruit will explode as it cooks. Whole baked apples should always be scored round the middle, plums should be halved or pierced with the prongs of a fork or scored with a knife. Small berries such as gooseberries must be pierced with the tip of a knife or the skins will split as they cook. Always undercook so the shape and texture of the fruit is retained. Cooking continues for a few minutes after the power has been turned off. This can be seen very clearly when baked apples are removed from the oven. The power should be turned off when the skins at each end of the apple are yellow and a central band of about ¾-1 inch (2-2.5cm) remains green. The standing time should be about 3 minutes, during which the band will gradually change colour as cooking continues. If necessary food can always be returned to the oven and cooked for a little longer.

The microwave can be extremely useful for blanching fresh fruit before freezing. As the availability of fruits is influenced by seasons this is a big advantage. It also defrosts fruit quickly and well. Frozen fruit should be defrosted on a low power level and frequently interrupted so the fruits can be gently separated with the prongs of a fork. The thawing process should be completed when the oven has been turned off; the heat generated within the fruit then continues thawing the food after it has been removed from the oven. One or two recipes using frozen fruit have been included in this section, but by following the chart opposite, fresh fruit may be used when in season. Look up the fruit and alter the cooking times accordingly.

The microwave can be used to remove the skins from fruit; microwave an apricot on HIGH for 6-8 seconds, leave to stand for 30 seconds and the skin can easily be peeled. It can also enable almost twice as much juice to be extracted from citrus fruits; microwave an orange on HIGH for 30 seconds and it will not only be easier to squeeze but will also yield far more juice. If a recipe requires the juice from several oranges, lemons or other citrus fruits the zests can be saved and used. They can be finely grated or removed in thin strips, sprinkled over a piece of kitchen paper, covered with a second sheet and cooked on HIGH for a few minutes. Check every 40 seconds and rub the zest between your fingers to separate the damp pieces. This same technique can be used to dry herbs. It is not advisable to dry very small quantities of zests or herbs.

By using a microwave oven it is possible to cook fruits for one or two people by methods which would otherwise be impractical: a single apple can be baked in about 2 minutes 30 seconds and a banana can be cooked in about 2 minutes. Simply slit the banana skin then place in the oven and cook on HIGH for 1-2 minutes until the skin has turned black – it is particularly delicious if ½oz (15g) of chocolate is pressed into the fruit so it is hidden beneath the skin. As the banana cooks the chocolate melts. Remember that the addition of ½oz (15g) chocolate to a banana will add 75 Calories.

Cooking Guidelines for Fruit

The condition of the fruit, its age and ripeness will affect its cooking time, but use the following as a guide. Stirring or rearranging may seem unnecessary but it does help to cook the fruit evenly. Cover the cooking dish with a lid or pierced clingfilm but make sure the film does not touch the fruit. Leave the fruit covered, to stand for 3 minutes. Sweeten the fruit after cooking.

Fruit & Weight	Setting	Time	Additional instructions
apples, sliced 8oz (240g)	HIGH	3 mins	Quarter, core and slice, stir once during cooking.
apples, baked 2 × 6oz (180g)	HIGH	4 mins	Remove the core and score all the way round the centre. Rearrange once during cooking and interrupt the cooking for about 30 seconds after 2 minutes 30 seconds.
apricots 8oz (240g)	HIGH	2 mins	Halve and remove the stones or score round each fruit, stir once during cooking.
berries – blackberries, raspberries & loganberries 8oz (240g)	HIGH	2 mins	Rinse, shake in a sieve, do not add any water, stir halfway through cooking.
cherries 8oz (240g)	HIGH	2 mins	Stone, add 1 tablespoon water, stir once during cooking.
currants – black, red & white 8oz (240g)	HIGH	3½ mins	Rinse, shake in a sieve, do not add any water, stir halfway through cooking.
damsons 8oz (240g)	HIGH	1½ mins	Halve and stone or score round each fruit. Add 2 tablespoons water, stir halfway through cooking.
gooseberries 8oz (240g)	HIGH	2 mins	Top and tail, pierce skins with the tip of the knife during preparation, add 1 tablespoon water, stir once during cooking.
greengages 8oz (240g)	HIGH	2 mins	Halve and stone or score round each fruit. Add 2 tablespoons water, stir once during cooking.
nectarines & peaches 8oz (240g)	HIGH	4 mins	Halve and stone, leave in halves or quarter or thickly slice. Add 2 tablespoons water, stir once during cooking.
pears, whole 2 × 4oz (120g)	HIGH	3 mins	Remove a very thin slice from base so they stand upright. Add 2 tablespoons water, rearrange halfway through cooking.
pears, sliced 8oz (240g)	HIGH	3 mins	Add 2 tablespoons water, stir once during cooking.
plums 8oz (240g) medium sized	HIGH	2 mins	Halve and stone or score round each fruit. Add 2 tablespoons water, stir once during cooking.
rhubarb 8oz (240g)	HIGH	3 mins	Cut into 1-1½ inch (2.5-4cm) lengths. Add 1 tablespoon water, stir once during cooking.
strawberries 8oz (240g)	HIGH	2 mins	Leave whole or halve large fruits if desired. Rinse and shake in a sieve, do not add water. Stir halfway through cooking.

Lemon Jelly with Raspberry Sauce

Serves 4
100 Calories per serving

Use a high-quality raspberry conserve or jam to make the sauce. Commercial conserves have a superior flavour compared with jams.

---

1 tablespoon cornflour

½ pint (300ml) skimmed milk

3 lemons

4oz (120g) fromage frais

artificial sweetener

few drops of yellow colouring (optional)

1 tablespoon gelatine

4oz (120g) raspberries

3 tablespoons sieved raspberry conserve

2 tablespoons low-fat natural yogurt

1 Blend the cornflour together with the milk.

2 Finely grate the zest from the lemons then squeeze to remove the juice. Stir the lemon zest into the milk mixture then cook, uncovered, on HIGH for 4 minutes. Stir every 40-50 seconds, until the sauce has thickened and is boiling.

3 Reserve 2 tablespoons lemon juice, gradually add the remainder to the hot sauce. Stir the warm mixture into the fromage frais and sweeten to taste with artificial sweetener. If desired add a few drops of yellow colouring.

4 Place the reserved lemon juice in a cup or small basin, sprinkle in the gelatine then cook, uncovered, on HIGH for 35 seconds. Stir well then leave until the gelatine has dissolved. Mix into the lemon sauce then pour into four small individual moulds and chill until set.

5 Sieve the raspberries. Gradually stir the raspberry juice into the sieved conserve.

6 To serve, dip the moulds briefly in hot water then invert onto individual serving plates and remove the moulds. Spoon the raspberry sauce round each jelly. Drizzle the yogurt over the sauce then, using the tip of a skewer, swirl the yogurt together with the sauce.

Selections per serving:
  ¼ Milk
  ½ Protein
  60 Optional Calories

Open Apple Pie

Serves 8
225 Calories per serving

This recipe is a substitute for the traditional double-crusted apple pie which cannot be successfully baked in a microwave oven.

---

1 × 8 inch (20cm) cooked flan case (see page 219)

1¼lb (600g) cooking apples

4 tablespoons water

1 teaspoon lemon juice

2oz (60g) wholemeal or white flour

good pinch of mixed spice

1oz (30g) margarine

1 tablespoon demerara sugar

½ teaspoon arrowroot

1 teaspoon granulated sugar

Selections per serving:
¾ Bread
2 Fat
½ Fruit
55 Optional Calories

1 Place the cooked flan case on a serving plate.

2 Peel, core, quarter then slice the apples. Place the apple slices, 4 tablespoons water and the lemon juice in a container. Cover and cook on HIGH for 2 minutes 40 seconds gently stirring halfway through the cooking time.

3 Sieve the flour and spice into a bowl, tip any bran remaining in the sieve into the bowl. Rub the margarine, if possible margarine which has been stored in the freezer, into the flour, then stir in the demerara sugar.

4 Using a slotted spoon remove the warm apple slices from the cooking container and arrange in the flan case.

5 Blend the cooking liquid from the apples with the arrowroot, pour into a small bowl and cook, uncovered, on HIGH for 1 minute 30 seconds, stirring halfway through the cooking time. Stir the granulated sugar into the arrowroot sauce and stir until dissolved then pour over the apples.

6 Sprinkle the flour mixture over the apples and cook, uncovered, on HIGH for 2 minutes 30 seconds. Stand for 2 minutes.

Peach and Pear Salad

Serves 4
85 Calories per serving

Peaches and nectarines are often sold firm and unsuitable for eating raw. This recipe is ideal for firm fruit but if the peaches are firm and the pears soft cook the peaches a little before adding the pears.

2 medium peaches or nectarines

2 medium pears

juice of ½ medium orange

2 teaspoons clear honey

5fl oz (150ml) low-fat natural yogurt

Selections per serving:
1 Fruit
¼ Milk
20 Optional Calories

1 Halve the peaches and remove the stones, cut each half in half again to give a total of eight quarters.

2 Peel the pears, cut them in half and remove the cores, then cut each half in half again.

3 Arrange the fruit in a large dish or on a plate with the thin ends of each pear quarter in the centre and overlapping other pieces of pear. Arrange the peach quarters between the pears, if necessary arrange the peaches two quarters with their skins down against the plate and then another quarter between them with the skin facing up.

4 Pour the orange juice over the fruit, cover and cook on HIGH for 4 minutes. Leave to stand for 1-2 minutes, then using a slotted spoon transfer the fruit to a serving dish or divide between four glass dishes.

5 Stir the honey into the hot orange juice, gradually stir in the yogurt and serve with the warm fruit.

VARIATION
Spread ¼oz (10g) flaked almonds evenly over a plate and cook on HIGH for 2 minutes or until light brown. Stir 1 or 2 drops of almond essence into the yogurt sauce then spoon over each portion of fruit. Sprinkle the toasted almonds over the top. Add an extra 15 Optional Calories to each portion.

Compôte of Dried Fruit

Serves 4
85 Calories per serving

6oz (180g) dried fruit – apple rings, apricots, peaches, pears

4fl oz (120ml) orange, apple or pineapple juice

6fl oz (180ml) water

¼ teaspoon ground ginger

zest of ¼ lemon

Selections per serving:
   1¾ Fruit

1   Place the dried fruit in a container, pour over the fruit juice and water.

2   Stir in the ginger. Remove the zest from the lemon with a zester or grate very finely then add to the dried fruit.

3   Cover the container and cook on HIGH for 6 minutes.

4   Stir the fruit, cover and cook on LOW for 12 minutes. Leave to stand for 5 minutes.

Calypso Bananas

Serves 4
105 Calories per serving

1 medium orange

¼ teaspoon ground cinnamon

1 teaspoon honey

4 medium bananas

1 tablespoon rum

Selections per serving:
   2 Fruit
   20 Optional Calories

1   Remove the orange zest with a zester or grate very finely.

2   Squeeze the juice from the orange and place in a bowl together with the orange zest, cinnamon and honey. Cover the bowl and cook on HIGH for 1 minute.

3   Cut the bananas in thick diagonal slices.

4   Stir the rum and sliced bananas into the hot orange juice, cover and cook for 2 minutes 30 seconds, stirring once during the cooking time. Stand for 2 minutes. Serve hot or cold.

Raspberry and Redcurrant Delight

Serves 2
85 Calories per serving

It's hard to believe that such a delicious refreshing dessert can be made in such a short time and using only two ingredients! The sharp tang of the raspberries is slightly sweetened with the redcurrant jelly. Don't serve it with any accompaniment or the flavour will be diluted and spoiled.

10oz (300g) frozen raspberries

2 tablespoons redcurrant jelly

1   Place the raspberries in a large container so they form a single layer.

2   Cover the dish, do not add any liquid, and cook on LOW for 2 minutes 30 seconds. Stir gently keeping the raspberries in a single layer.

3   Cover the dish and return to the oven. Cook on LOW for 1 minute then remove from the oven and stir once again.

4   Add the redcurrant jelly in teaspoons to coat as many raspberries as possible.

5   Cover the dish and cook on LOW for 1 minute, stir then cover and cook for 40-50 seconds. The raspberries should be slightly warm, whole and separate and the redcurrant jelly should be evenly melted over the fruit.

6   Spoon the fruit into two serving glasses. Serve within 1 hour or the raspberries will collapse and the amount of liquid increase.

Selections per serving:
  1 Fruit
  50 Optional Calories

Butterscotch Pears

Serves 2
90 Calories per serving

Don't worry if the pears discolour a little after cooking, the sauce is light brown
and will disguise any browning.

---

2 medium pears

lemon juice

½ tablespoon golden syrup

½ tablespoon soft brown sugar

1 teaspoon margarine

½ teaspoon hot water

1 Peel the pears. Cut a thin slice from the base of each pear so it stands upright.

2 Brush the pears generously with lemon juice and place in a container which will allow them to stand upright below the top of the dish.

3 Add 2 tablespoons water to the dish, cover and cook on HIGH for 2 minutes then rearrange and cook for 1 minute – the time will vary according to the ripeness of the pears so check every following 20 seconds. Leave the pears to cool.

4 Spoon the syrup, sugar and margarine into a small bowl. Cook, uncovered, on HIGH for 40 seconds – the mixture is very high in sugar and fat so the bowl will be hot. Stir the mixture well then return to the oven and cook on HIGH for 30 seconds. Immediately add the hot water and stir well. Leave to cool.

Selections per serving:
  ½ Fat
  1 Fruit
  30 Optional Calories

5 Serve the pears standing upright on individual plates and pour the sauce over the top so it runs from the stalk to the plate.

Mixed Fruit Kebabs

Serves 4
175 Calories per serving

These kebabs make a refreshing and unusual end to a meal. If you wish, substitute the papaya with half a medium mango or replace the banana with a medium peach and a juicy pear.

½ **medium papaya**

1 medium banana

3oz (90g) large black grapes

½ small avocado (3oz/90g)

4oz (120g) fresh or drained canned pineapple

1½ tablespoons maple syrup

2 teaspoons lemon juice

10fl oz (300ml) low-fat natural yogurt

Selections per serving:
  ¾ Fat
  1 Fruit
  ½ Milk
  35 Optional Calories

1   Scoop out and discard the seeds from the papaya. Remove the peel and cut the flesh into twelve cubes.

2   Peel and thickly slice the banana.

3   Halve the grapes then remove the seeds.

4   Remove the avocado skin and cut the flesh into ¾ inch (2cm) cubes.

5   Cut the pineapple into chunks about the same size as the papaya.

6   Stir 1 teaspoon maple syrup together with the lemon juice. Toss the prepared fruit in the lemon juice mixture then thread onto eight wooden skewers.

7   Lay the Fruit Kebabs on a plate, cover with an upturned basin and cook on HIGH for 2 minutes 30 seconds. Leave to stand for 1 minute.

8   Stir the remaining maple syrup into the yogurt. Transfer the cooked kebabs to four individual serving plates and tip any cooking juices into the yogurt. Serve the kebabs with the maple yogurt.

Grapefruit Cups

Serves 2
85 Calories per serving

This recipe can be served as a starter or dessert. The pink-skinned grapefruit is ideal as it is sweeter than the other varieties.

1 medium grapefruit – preferably pink-skinned

½ medium orange

2 tablespoons sweet sherry

1½ teaspoons caster sugar

1 Make several 'V' shaped cuts around the grapefruit, deep enough to reach the centre of the fruit.

2 Gently pull the grapefruit halves apart, if they don't easily separate make the cuts a little deeper.

3 Using a grapefruit knife remove all the grapefruit segments but do not break the skin. Chop the grapefruit into large pieces removing any particularly tough membranes.

4 Divide the orange segments. Remove as much membrane as possible from each of the segments then cut in half and add to the chopped grapefruit.

5 Mix the sherry together with 1 teaspoon sugar, pour over the prepared fruit and stir round.

6 Spoon the orange and grapefruit into the grapefruit skins, spoon the sherry syrup over and sprinkle each half with the remaining sugar.

7 Transfer the Grapefruit Cups to a plate, cover with an upturned bowl and cook on HIGH for 2 minutes. Leave to stand for 2 minutes.

Selections per serving:
  1¼ Fruit
  50 Optional Calories

Pear Soup

Serves 2
180 Calories per serving

Fruit soups are popular on the continent but not often served in Great Britain. This recipe makes a refreshing start to a meal – don't be tempted to add any sweetening as it should be slightly sharp.

1lb (480g) peeled pears, quartered and cored

8fl oz (240ml) white wine

2 inch (5cm) strip lemon zest

1 tablespoon lemon juice

2 inch (5cm) stick cinnamon

3 or 4 ice cubes, crushed

Selections per serving:
  2 Fruit
  100 Optional Calories

1 Roughly chop the pears, place in a container with the wine, lemon zest and juice.

2 Break the cinnamon between your fingers, just enough to form a few splinters. Add the cinnamon to the pears and lemon juice, cover and cook on HIGH for 10 minutes.

3 Leave the pears in their cooking liquid until cool then remove the larger pieces of cinnamon, leave a few of the smaller pieces, and the lemon zest.

4 Transfer the pears and their cooking liquid to a liquidiser and process to form a purée. Chill the soup until it is to be served.

5 Pour the soup into two cold serving dishes, add a few crushed ice cubes then serve immediately.

Stuffed Apples

Serves 2
125 Calories per serving

Baked apples can be a disaster when cooked in the microwave but I have found the method below gives very good results.

2 × 6oz (180g) cooking apples

1oz (30g) raisins or sultanas

2 teaspoons honey

1   Using an apple corer remove the core from the apples. Cut two or three times into the apples to ensure all the core has been removed. Cut a thin piece of apple skin from the edge of each end where the core has been removed.

2   Score each apple around the centre, between the core ends.

3   Place the apples in individual dishes or ramekins and cook, uncovered, on HIGH for 2 minutes 30 seconds.

4   Remove apples from the oven, turn upside down and halfway round. Leave out of the oven for 30 seconds while piling the dried fruit into the core cavity.

5   Return to the oven and cook, uncovered, on HIGH for 50 seconds. The apples should be yellow at each end but a centre band, about ¾-1 inch (2-2.5cm) should still be green.

6   Cover the apples and leave for 3 minutes – by this time the apple should be completely cooked and the skin yellow. If necessary return to the oven but only cook for 30 seconds or the dried fruit will be pushed out by apple pulp. Pour the honey over the dried fruit and serve.

To bake one apple: halve the quantities above and cook, uncovered, for 1 minute 30 seconds, turn upside down and halfway round then cook for 30 seconds. Leave covered for 3 minutes.

Selections per serving:
   1½ Fruit
   20 Optional Calories

Tangy Chocolate Sundae

Serves 6
120 Calories per serving

If you prefer, substitute other canned fruits such as pears or apricots.

---

2 medium oranges

1 tablespoon cornflour

1¾oz (50g) milk chocolate

2 teaspoons caster sugar

8oz (240g) fromage frais

1lb (480g) mixture of drained canned pineapple and mandarin segments

Selections per serving:
1 Fruit
½ Protein
60 Optional Calories

1 Finely grate the zest from half an orange, squeeze the juice from both the oranges.

2 Blend the cornflour to a smooth paste with a little of the orange juice, stir in the remaining juice and place the mixture in a bowl. Cook, uncovered, on HIGH for 3 minutes stirring every 40-50 seconds.

3 Grate the chocolate and put a little – just sufficient for decorating the desserts – aside.

4 Allow the orange sauce to cool for 3-4 minutes, add the sugar and grated chocolate and stir until melted. Stir in the fromage frais then leave until cold.

5 Just before serving, spoon the fruit into six tall slim glasses, spoon the orange and chocolate sauce over and decorate with the reserved grated chocolate.

Strawberry Jelly

Serves 4
90 Calories per serving

This is a simple dessert which may be served at a luncheon or dinner party. It can be made well in advance and stored in the refrigerator. Although it is best made with really fresh sweet strawberries the frozen fruit may be substituted: defrost a little in the microwave before proceeding with the recipe, then thaw the fruit to surround the jellies just before serving.

1lb 12oz (840g) strawberries

1 medium orange

4½ teaspoons caster sugar

1 sachet gelatine

Selections per serving:
  1½ Fruit
  30 Optional Calories

1   Reserve 12oz (360g) strawberries for decoration, place the remainder in a liquidiser and process to a purée.

2   Squeeze the juice from the orange then pour into a cup or small basin, add 4 teaspoons sugar and sprinkle in the gelatine. Heat the juice on HIGH for 50 seconds.

3   Stir the hot orange juice mixture until the sugar and gelatine have dissolved. If necessary, return the juice to the oven and reheat on HIGH for a few seconds.

4   Stir the orange juice into the strawberry purée and pour into four individual moulds. Chill until completely set.

5   To serve; dip the moulds in warm water then immediately invert onto serving plates. Cut all the reserved strawberries in half, place in a bowl and sprinkle over the remaining sugar, mix well. Decorate the top of each jelly with half a strawberry and arrange the remainder around them.

All Hallows Pudding

Serves 4
85 Calories per serving

It is surprising how much the skin and seeds of the pumpkin weigh, allow just under one pound (480g) wastage from half a pumpkin weighing about 2¼-2½lb (1.1-1.2kg).

1½lb (720g) pumpkin, seeds and skin removed

finely grated zest and juice of 1 medium orange

1½ inch (4cm) stick cinnamon

2oz (60g) dried stoned dates

4oz (120g) fromage frais

Selections per serving:
  ¾ Fruit
  ½ Protein
  2 Vegetable

1 Dice the pumpkin and place in a container with the orange zest and juice. Crumble the cinnamon into the dish and stir round.

2 Cover the dish and cook on HIGH for 10 minutes, stirring halfway through the cooking time.

3 Finely chop the dates.

4 Place the pumpkin and dates in a liquidiser and process to a thick purée. Allow to cool.

5 Stir the fromage frais unevenly through the pumpkin purée and divide between four serving glasses.

Pineberry Mousse

Serves 4
155 Calories per serving

This dessert retains the tang of the pineapple and raspberries. Don't substitute the fresh raspberries with frozen or canned varieties as their red juice would run and prevent the mixture setting. The set is very weak and wouldn't be suitable for setting in a mould, it is just sufficient to hold the raspberries in the mixture.

---

1 × 15¼oz (432g) can crushed pineapple

2 medium oranges

6 tablespoons single cream

1 tablespoon gelatine

12oz (360g) raspberries

Selections per serving:
  2 Fruit
  75 Optional Calories

1 Pour the crushed pineapple into the goblet of a liquidiser.

2 Squeeze the juice from the oranges. Place about 3 tablespoons orange juice in a cup or small basin, add the remainder to the liquidiser. Liquidise the pineapple and orange juice until evenly mixed then add the cream and process again.

3 Sprinkle the gelatine into the reserved orange, stir well then place in the oven and cook, uncovered, on HIGH for 45 seconds. Stir the hot orange juice and gelatine until dissolved, if necessary return to the oven for a few more seconds. Pour the dissolved gelatine into the liquidiser and process once again.

4 Pour the fruit purée into a bowl and chill until thick and beginning to set.

5 Wash the raspberries then pat dry with kitchen paper. Fold the raspberries into the setting mixture then spoon into four serving glasses. Chill for 1-2 hours.

Hot Fruit Salad

Serves 4
65 Calories per serving

Cold fruit salads are sometimes served in melon or pineapple skins but this recipe is unusual as the microwave oven makes it possible to serve hot fruit in a fruit basket. Use a really fresh pineapple so the leaves don't brown during cooking.

1 medium pineapple

½ medium mango

1 large fig

2 teaspoons soft brown sugar

1   Cut the pineapple in half. Using a grapefruit knife scoop out as much of the fruit as possible but leave the skin intact. Reserve all the juice which drips from the pineapple during preparation.

2   Cut the pineapple and mango into 1 inch (2.5cm) cubes. Thickly slice the fig.

3   Arrange the fruit in each pineapple half.

4   Mix the reserved juice with the brown sugar and spoon over the fruit.

5   Place one half of the filled pineapple on a plate, cover with an upturned bowl and cook on HIGH for 2 minutes 30 seconds. Remove from the oven and repeat with the other half, leave to stand for 5 minutes.

Selections per serving:
  1½ Fruit
  20 Optional Calories

Cranberry Fool

Serves 2
100 Calories per serving

Don't overcook the cranberries for this recipe, there should be a few slightly firm berries.

8oz (240g) cranberries

1 tablespoon custard powder

¼ pint (150ml) skimmed milk

artificial sweetener

5fl oz (150ml) low-fat natural yogurt

Selections per serving:
  ¾ Fruit
  ¾ Milk
  15 Optional Calories

1 Place the cranberries in a container, add 1 tablespoon water. Cover the container and cook on HIGH for 2 minutes 30 seconds.

2 Blend the custard powder together with the milk.

3 Place the custard in the oven and cook, uncovered, on HIGH for 3 minutes stirring every minute until boiling and thick.

4 Mash the cranberries unevenly with a fork, leave a few whole.

5 Stir the cranberries into the warm custard and sweeten to taste with artificial sweetener. Leave until cool.

6 Stir the yogurt into the cool cranberry custard and chill until ready to serve.

Plum and Apple Crumble

Serves 4
235 Calories per serving

This recipe contains dessert apples and sweet plums therefore no additional sweetening is required. The crumble topping is made with wholemeal flour and contains a little demerara sugar so it resembles the traditional golden coloured crumble. If you prefer, use white flour and sugar.

1lb (480g) sweet plums

2 medium dessert apples

1½oz (45g) margarine

3oz (90g) wholemeal flour

1 tablespoon demerara sugar

Selections per serving:
  ¾ Bread
  2 Fat
  1½ Fruit
  25 Optional Calories

1   Halve the plums and remove the stones. If the plums are large, cut each half into two or three wedges.

2   Peel, quarter and core the apples then cut into thin slices.

3   Place a layer of plums over the base of a 6 inch (15cm) deep container, arrange the apple slices in a layer on top of the plums then cover with the remaining plums. Cover the dish and cook on HIGH for 5-6 minutes or until the fruit is almost cooked but still a little firm. Turn the dish 180 degrees halfway through the cooking time.

4   Rub the margarine, if possible margarine which has been stored in the freezer, into the flour then stir in the sugar.

5   Sprinkle the crumble topping evenly over the hot fruit. Return to the oven and cook, uncovered, on HIGH for 4 minutes. Leave to stand for 3 minutes.

Plum and Apple Crumble with Custard (see page 84)

Three Fruit Marmalade

Makes approximately 4lb (1.9kg)
50 Calories per tablespoon

Marmalade made in the microwave differs from the conventional variety in several ways: the pips are not placed in muslin and boiled in the fruit juices; it is not possible to make such large quantities – but nowadays less marmalade is eaten so this need not be a disadvantage; it does not require a large heavy-based pan – a large glass bowl is ideal; it is made in a fairly short time and it has a cloudy appearance, unlike the clear jelly of a traditional marmalade.

1 medium grapefruit

2 medium oranges } **total weight 2½lb (1.2kg)**

3 lemons

2lb (960g) granulated sugar

½ tablespoon butter

1 Using a potato peeler remove the zest from the fruit then set aside.

2 Roughly chop the fruit and white pith and place, together with the pips, in a food processor.

3 Liquidise until the fruit is a thick purée and the pips have broken into small pieces.

4 Pour the fruit purée into a large glass bowl, pour over 1½ pints (900ml) boiling water and place in the microwave. Cook, uncovered, on HIGH for 20 minutes.

5 While the fruit pulp is cooking cut the zests into very fine strips.

6 Using oven gloves, carefully remove the bowl of boiling pulp from the oven.

7 Sieve the pulp into a clean bowl by pushing the mixture hard against the sides of the sieve with a wooden spoon, then by scraping it from the underside of the sieve with a metal spoon. Take time over this as it is important to remove as much of the liquid from the mixture as possible – only a few tablespoons of very thick pulp should remain in the sieve.

8   Stir the zest into the sieved mixture and return to the microwave. Cook, uncovered, on HIGH for 15 minutes or until the zest is soft.

9   Add the sugar and stir until completely dissolved. Cover the bowl with clingfilm then fold back about a quarter of the film to allow steam to escape. Return the bowl to the oven and cook on HIGH for 13 minutes, stirring twice during the cooking time.

10 Stir in the butter and spoon a little of the marmalade onto a chilled plate, place in the refrigerator for a few minutes and when cool test for setting; gently push the marmalade with a finger, if the setting point has been reached the surface will wrinkle and slightly lift as the finger is removed from the plate. If the setting point has not been reached return to the oven and cook on HIGH for 30-60 seconds then repeat the test until a set is attained. Remember to stop cooking the marmalade while testing the set.

11 Leave the marmalade to stand for 15 minutes then transfer to the sterilized jars (see recipe for Strawberry Jam), cover and leave until cold, then label.

Selections per serving:
   50 Optional Calories
   per tablespoon

Strawberry Jam

Makes approximatey 2¼lb (1.1kg)
50 Calories per tablespoon

When strawberries are cheap and in plentiful supply make this jam then store it in a cool dark cupboard until it is to be used. Strawberries are low in pectin, the setting agent in fruit, therefore lemon juice is added to the berries. Never use over-ripe fruit when making jam.

1½lb (720g) strawberries

1lb (480g) granulated sugar

5 tablespoons lemon juice

½ tablespoon butter

1   First of all sterilise the jam jars. Quarter fill the jars with water and cook on HIGH until the water is boiling. Using oven gloves carefully remove the jars from the oven. Tip out the water and turn upside down onto a clean cloth. Leave until completely dry.

2   Halve or thickly slice about 1lb (480g) strawberries, place in a large glass bowl and stir in the sugar. Cover the bowl and leave to stand for 5-6 hours until the berries have softened and are covered by a syrup.

3   Stir the lemon juice into the strawberries and sugar, place the bowl in the oven and cook, uncovered, on LOW for 15-20 minutes, stirring two or three times during cooking, until the sugar has completely dissolved.

4   Stir the butter into the strawberry mixture and cook, uncovered, on HIGH for 32-33 minutes then test the set. Place a teaspoon of jam on a cold saucer and leave until cool then with a finger gently push the jam across the saucer. If it wrinkles and rises slightly as the finger is removed setting point has been reached. If it has not reached setting point cook for a further 30-60 seconds depending how weak the set, then test once again.

Selections per serving:
   50 Optional Calories
   per tablespoon

5   Leave the jam to cool for 15 minutes. Spoon or pour the jam into the jars then seal. Leave to cool then label.

Baking

Microwave cakes and breads look very different from conventionally baked mixtures. As there is no dry heat they do not have a crust or a golden brown colour. Don't compare microwaved breads and cakes with traditional recipes, their texture and appearance will be different, they should be enjoyed for what they are and not what they would have been had they been baked by other methods.

CAKES, BISCUITS AND SCONES

It is possible to cook many cakes successfully in the microwave but biscuits are not so satisfactory as they do not become crisp. Biscuits such as Flapjacks and the Crispy Ginger Baskets which are included in this section are made by the 'melting method' – when fat is melted with sugar and syrup, and this method produces very good results.

Microwave cooked scones are spongier than traditional ones and do not have a crisp crust. Cook on a very hot browning griddle and eat them while they are still warm. Always reheat the griddle after cooking one batch of scones as it cools quickly. Sponge cakes, small buns and fruit cakes can all be made successfully in the microwave but it will take practice to obtain consistently good results. Before dashing out and buying the special microwave cookware look through your cupboards; many china, pottery and glass dishes make good baking dishes. The following few basic rules should be followed when baking cakes.

1 Choose a deep cake dish to allow plenty of room for the cake to rise, the mixture should only half fill the dish. Never use a dish which is more than 8 inches (20cm) in diameter or the middle will be damp. Ring moulds are particularly well suited to microwave cooking as they enable the microwaves to penetrate from the middle as well as the outer edge, top and bottom. Whenever possible avoid the use of square and rectangular dishes.

2 Line the dish with non-stick baking parchment or grease lightly, do not grease then flour the dish or the flour will cook and form an unpleasant crust.

3 Cakes made by the 'creaming' or 'rubbing in' methods – when the fat and sugar are creamed or rubbed into the dry ingredients – should be mixed with more liquid than usual. Allow an extra 2-3 teaspoons liquid per egg. The mixture should be slacker than normal and drop easily from a spoon when gently tapped against the side of the dish. The fat and sugar must always be evenly distributed throughout the mixture as they attract microwaves and lumps would cause burning.

4 Dried fruit doesn't have sufficient time to absorb moisture during baking. This is not very important in small cakes when the cooking time is short but when making a fruit cake the fruit should be soaked or cooked a little. Either soak or cook the fruit in water, tea or fruit juice then drain before adding to the cake mixture – if the cake is to be baked immediately it doesn't matter if the fruit is still warm. Even with the addition of soaked fruit the mixture may be too dry, if so add a little of the soaking or cooking liquid.

5 Don't over-mix or add too much raising agent as microwaved cakes rise well.

6 By placing the cooking dish on a rack in the oven, the microwaves have easier access to the dish. If you don't have a rack, stand the dish on an upturned plate or saucer. Arrange small cakes in a circle, do not place them in the centre or they will not cook evenly.

7 Never cover a biscuit or cake mixture or the result will be a very moist texture similar to a steamed pudding.

8 Cook layered cakes, such as sponge cakes, in a single deep container then split in two or three after baking.

9 Probably the most important decision when baking is when to remove the cake from the oven. Mixtures must not be over-cooked or they will be extremely dry and possibly inedible, this is a very common mistake. Cakes must be removed from the oven while they still look slightly moist. Cooking should be completed during the standing time when the top should dry and the cake shrink a little from the edge of the dish. Standing time will vary from one cake to another, some rich fruit cakes require 15-20 minutes. After the stated standing time, turn the cake out of the dish and remove the lining paper – if the cake is still damp on the bottom, place it upside down on a piece of non-stick baking parchment then return to the oven and place on the turntable, not the rack, and cook for a short time. By positioning the cake on the turntable the microwaves will be directed towards the damp patch.

BREAD

A microwave oven can be used to speed up traditional bread-making processes; the dry ingredients can be warmed and the dough can be proved and risen by short bursts of microwave energy. It is possible to bake a yeast bread dough in the microwave and a recipe for a plain loaf is included in this section. However, as there is no dry heat the bread will not have the traditional crust. The texture is not as airy as a traditional loaf and the air holes tend to be small and dense. If you wish to cook the bread dough as rolls, bake about six rolls at a time and cook on HIGH for 2-3 minutes, repositioning once during the cooking time. The great advantage is the speed at which the bread can be made and the ease with which it can be cut very soon after baking.

White bread looks rather anaemic and un-appetising but wholemeal bread has an agreeable appearance and a firmer texture than bread cooked in the traditional way. To obtain a crust on loaves or rolls place them under a preheated grill for a short time, turning frequently, so the crust is even all the way round the bread.

Soda bread can be baked very success-fully in the microwave. The texture is good and as it is traditionally eaten very fresh, while still warm, there is no problem concerning the bread drying during storage. If all the bread is not eaten while fresh it can be frozen then thawed and reheated in the microwave when required.

PASTRY

Shortcrust pastry can be baked success-fully in the microwave oven but it does not have such a good texture as conventionally cooked pastry. Puff pastry rises dramatically during baking and, even when the oven door is opened the pastry is not spoiled – immediately the power is turned on it rises again. It is more difficult to judge when the pastry is cooked than conventionally baked pastry as it does not turn golden brown. The cooked pastry should hold its shape and be crisp.

Shortcrust pastry can be used to make flan cases but it is not possible to make a double crusted pie. Flan cases may be baked blind or the pastry can be lined with non-stick baking parchment with a few baking beans to weigh down the middle. If you choose to use baking beans they should be removed about 1 minute before the end of the cooking time to allow time for the centre of the flan to dry out. I haven't found it necessary to use beans but if you are particularly heavy-handed and stretch the pastry as you roll it out they could be useful to keep the pastry in shape. A recipe for making a pastry flan case is included in this section. Never attempt to make a flan case larger than 8 inches (20cm) in diameter and always cook in circular, uncovered dishes. Cook in the same way as cakes and breads, on a rack or upturned plate.

Flans can be reheated successfully but place the cooked flan on a double thickness of kitchen paper to prevent it becoming moist.

Soda Bread

Makes 1 loaf

Soda bread should be eaten while still warm. It does not keep well and any bread which is not to be eaten on the same day as baking should be frozen. It freezes quite well and can be thawed and warmed in a short time with the use of the microwave oven. As buttermilk is sold in half pints I suggest a little skimmed milk is incorporated if the dough is too dry. However, if you have extra buttermilk, omit the milk.

1lb (480g) wholemeal flour (or a mixture of half wholemeal and half white)

1 teaspoon salt

2 teaspoons bicarbonate of soda

1oz (30g) margarine

½ pint (300ml) buttermilk

skimmed milk

1 Reserve 1 tablespoon flour and sieve the remainder with the salt and bicarbonate of soda into a bowl. Tip any bran remaining in the sieve into the bowl.

2 Rub the margarine, if possible margarine which has been stored in the freezer, into the flour.

3 Add the buttermilk and mix to form a soft dough, if necessary add a little more skimmed milk or buttermilk.

4 Flour a working surface with the reserved flour. Turn the dough onto the work surface and knead until smooth.

5 Lay a piece of non-stick baking parchment on a microwave roasting trivet and press the dough out until about 7 inches (17.5cm) round. Using a sharp knife cut the dough about a third of the way through to divide it into four.

6 Cook on HIGH for 8 minutes 30 seconds. Turn the bread carefully upside down and return to the oven for 1 minute 30 seconds. If the base feels damp place under a hot grill for 30-40 seconds, do not allow it to brown. Place the bread the right way up on a cooling rack and allow to cool until just warm. Serve immediately or wrap in a clean teacloth until it is to be served. Serve alone or with a sweet or savoury accompaniment.

Selections per serving:
   1oz (30g) slice = 1 Bread

Wholemeal Bread

Makes 1 loaf

A microwave-baked loaf has a firmer texture than traditional bread – this can be an advantage as it is possible to slice the loaf thinly while very fresh.

½ pint (300ml) skimmed milk

1 teaspoon sugar

1 tablespoon dried yeast

1lb (480g) strong wholemeal flour

½ teaspoon salt

1½oz (45g) margarine

1   Pour the milk into a measuring jug and heat on HIGH for about 1 minute 30 seconds until hand hot.

2   Stir the sugar into the warm milk then sprinkle in the yeast and, using a fork, whisk until dissolved. Leave for 10-15 minutes until a ½-1 inch (1.25-2.5cm) froth has formed on the surface.

3   Sieve the flour and salt into a bowl, tip the bran remaining in the sieve into the bowl.

4   Grease an 8½ × 4½ inch (21.5×11.25cm) loaf dish with a little of the margarine.

5   Rub the remaining margarine into the flour. Place the rubbed in mixture in the oven and heat on HIGH for 30 seconds.

6   Using a wooden spoon mix the frothy milk into the warm flour and continue mixing until the mixture becomes a firm ball.

7   Tip the dough onto the work surface and knead until it forms a tight ball. Shape into an oblong then place in the bowl.

8   Cover the dough with a very slightly damp tea towel and microwave on HIGH for 5 seconds, leave for 15 minutes. Then microwave for 5 more seconds and leave for 15 minutes.

9   When the dough has doubled in size tip it onto a work surface and knead once again.

10 Roll the dough into an oblong, place in the loaf dish and press down. Cover with the very slightly damp tea towel and microwave on HIGH for 5 seconds, leave covered until the dough has risen just above the level of the dish.

Selections per serving:
   1oz (30g) slice = 1 Bread

11 Return the bread to the oven and cook on HIGH for 5 minutes 30 seconds – 6 minutes until the loaf feels just firm. Do not overcook.

12 Check the loaf is cooked by inserting a cocktail stick into the centre – the bread is cooked if the stick is removed and remains clean. Leave in the dish for 10-15 minutes.

13 Turn the loaf out of the dish then transfer to a cooling rack, or brown for a short time under a preheated grill.

Scones

Serves 8
165 Calories per scone

Scones made in the microwave oven don't have the same texture as traditional scones cooked on a griddle or in the oven. Eat the scones while still warm and don't cook them for too long or they will dry.

8oz (240g) plain flour

¼ teaspoon salt

2½ teaspoons baking powder

1½oz (45g) margarine

1½oz (45g) sultanas

¼ pint (150ml) skimmed milk

Selections per serving:
1 Bread
1 Fat
25 Optional Calories

1 Reserve about 2 teaspoons of flour. Sieve the remainder, together with the salt and baking powder, into a bowl.

2 Rub the margarine, if possible margarine which has been stored in the freezer, into the flour.

3 Stir the sultanas into the flour then add the milk. Mix with a round-bladed knife to form a soft but not sticky dough.

4 Dust a working surface with a little of the reserved flour. Gently roll out the dough until about ¾ inch (2cm) thick. Using a 1½ inch (4cm) round cutter cut out eight scones, rerolling the dough only once.

5 Leave the scones for 10-15 minutes.

6 Preheat the browning griddle for 5-6 minutes or according to the manufacturers instructions.

7 Transfer the scones to the hot griddle and cook on HIGH for 1 minute 30 seconds. Carefully turn the scones over and cook on HIGH for a further 3 minutes 30 seconds.

8 Transfer the scones to a cooling rack and leave until warm. Serve while fresh and warm.

Flapjack

Serves 15
130 Calories per serving

Biscuits made by melting fat together with sugar and syrup cook very well in the microwave, but remember to place the dish on a rack or upturned plate and adjust the times according to the power of your oven.

3oz (90g) margarine

2oz (60g) soft brown sugar

2 tablespoons golden syrup

¾ teaspoon ground mixed spice or ginger (optional)

7½oz (225g) porridge oats

Selections per serving:
  ½ Bread
  1 Fat
  30 Optional Calories

1 Line a dish approximately 6 × 9 inches (15×22.5cm) with non-stick baking parchment.

2 Place the margarine, sugar, syrup and spice in a bowl and microwave, uncovered, on HIGH for 1 minute 20 seconds, stir well. Stir until the margarine has melted and the sugar dissolved.

3 Stir the porridge oats into the syrup mixture. Transfer the mixture to the prepared dish and press evenly and firmly over the dish using the back of a spoon.

4 Place the dish on a rack in the oven and microwave uncovered on HIGH for 3 minutes 30 seconds.

5 Remove from the oven and leave to stand for 2 minutes then mark into fifteen pieces. Leave in the dish until cold then cut all the way through the Flapjack and remove from the dish.

Gingerbread

Serves 12
120 Calories per serving

If you prefer, white plain flour may be used instead of wholemeal.

6oz (180g) plain wholemeal flour

½ teaspoon baking powder

1 teaspoon bicarbonate of soda

1½ teaspoons ground ginger

½ teaspoon mixed spice

2oz (60g) margarine

1½oz (45g) soft brown sugar

3 tablespoons golden syrup

1 egg

5 tablespoons water

Selections per serving:
  ½ Bread
  1 Fat
  35 Optional Calories

1   Line a shallow dish about 9 × 6 inches (22.5×15cm) with non-stick baking parchment.

2   Sieve the flour, baking powder, bicarbonate of soda, ginger and mixed spice into a bowl, tip the bran remaining in the sieve into the bowl then set aside.

3   Place the margarine, sugar and syrup in a separate bowl. Heat on MEDIUM for 1 minute 40 seconds, stir well to combine.

4   Lightly beat the egg with the water.

5   Tip the sieved flour and egg into the margarine mixture and stir well.

6   Pour the thick batter into the prepared dish and tilt from side to side to distribute the mixture evenly.

7   Cook, uncovered, on MEDIUM for 3 minutes 30 seconds then on HIGH for 2 minutes. If your oven doesn't have a turntable rotate the dish frequently to prevent it cooking unevenly.

Chocolate Pudding with White Sauce

Serves 4
295 Calories per serving

A steamed sponge pudding takes about 1½ hours to cook, but this pudding is made and cooked in 10 minutes.

For the pudding:

1½oz (45g) margarine

1½oz (45g) caster sugar

1 teaspoon golden syrup

1 egg, lightly beaten

3oz (90g) self-raising flour

1 tablespoon cocoa

2 tablespoons water

For the sauce:

2 tablespoons cornflour

½ pint (300ml) skimmed milk

1 tablespoon caster sugar

¼ teaspoon vanilla essence

Selections per serving:
  ¾ Bread
  2 Fat
  ¼ Milk
  115 Optional Calories

1   Grease a 2 pint (1.2 litre) basin with ½-1 teaspoon margarine from the measured amount and set aside.

2   Cream the remaining margarine and sugar until light and fluffy. Beat in the golden syrup then gradually beat in about half the egg.

3   Sieve the flour together with the cocoa.

4   Fold the flour and cocoa, remaining egg and water into the creamed mixture.

5   Spoon the chocolate pudding mixture into the prepared bowl and cover with a pleated piece of pierced clingfilm. Pull the film up to make a 'tent' above the bowl.

6   Cook on HIGH for 3 minutes 45 seconds. Allow to stand for 2 minutes while making the sauce.

7   Blend the cornflour together with the milk, stir in the sugar and vanilla essence and place, uncovered, in the oven.

8   Cook on HIGH for 3 minutes 30 seconds until boiling and thick. Stir three times during cooking.

9   Remove the clingfilm from the pudding then turn out onto a serving plate. Serve with the white sauce.

Crispy Ginger Baskets

Serves 6
175 Calories per serving

These fruit-filled baskets make an attractive dessert. Fill them only a short while before serving, otherwise the biscuit basket will soften.

2 tablespoons golden syrup

1oz (30g) soft brown sugar

1oz (30g) margarine

1oz (30g) plain flour

½ teaspoon ground ginger

1 medium banana

4oz (120g) fromage frais (8% fat)

¼-½ teaspoon lemon juice

2 medium mangoes

2 kiwi fruit

1 Place the syrup, sugar and margarine in a bowl. Sieve the flour and ginger into a separate bowl then set aside.

2 Place the bowl containing the syrup mixture into the oven and cook on MEDIUM for 1 minute 40 seconds, stir well then add the flour and ginger and mix until evenly blended.

3 Lay a 6 inch (15cm) circle of non-stick baking parchment on the oven turntable. Spoon about one-sixth of the syrup mixture onto the centre of the paper and cook on HIGH for about 1 minute until the mixture has spread and is a bubbling dark golden colour. Slide the paper carefully off the turntable and continue cooking the mixture by the same method.

4 Allow each biscuit to cool on the paper for 1-2 minutes then gently lift the edges of the circle and transfer to an upturned small basin or round-bottomed cup. Lay the biscuit over the base of the bowl and cup and very gently and lightly press the edge down. Leave until completely cold.

5 Just before serving mash the banana together with the fromage frais, add a little lemon juice to taste. Halve then dice the mangoes and slice the kiwi fruit, then cut each slice in two or three pieces.

6 Spoon the fromage frais mixture into each ginger biscuit basket and arrange the mango and kiwi fruit on top.

Selections per serving:
   1 Fat
   1¼ Fruit
   ¼ Protein
   60 Optional Calories

Christmas Pudding

Serves 8
240 Calories per serving

It is always hard to lose, or even maintain, weight at Christmas time but try making this pudding instead of the traditional heavy sweet suet pudding. The mixture doesn't require any added fat, use only a small amount to grease the basin. As it doesn't keep well either mix it on Christmas Eve then cook on Christmas Day or make one or two days in advance, cover and store in the refrigerator then reheat on Christmas Day.

4oz (120g) currants

4oz (120g) sultanas

4oz (120g) raisins

¼ pint (150ml) skimmed milk

½ teaspoon margarine

grated zest of 1 lemon

6oz (180g) breadcrumbs

2oz (60g) flour

½ teaspoon allspice

½ teaspoon cinnamon

1oz (30g) soft brown sugar

1½oz (45g) carrot, grated

2 eggs, size 2

1 tablespoon treacle

1½ teaspoons brandy flavouring

1-1½ teaspoons gravy browning (2-3 teaspoons if using white breadcrumbs and flour)

1   Place the dried fruit in a bowl.

2   Heat the milk on HIGH for 1 minute 30 seconds, pour over the dried fruit, stir round then leave for 30-40 minutes.

3   Grease a 2 pint (1.2 litre) pudding basin with the margarine.

4   Stir the lemon zest together with the breadcrumbs, flour, spices, sugar and carrot.

5   Lightly whisk the eggs together with the treacle, brandy flavouring and gravy browning.

6   Add the fruit, any remaining milk and the beaten egg mixture to the dry ingredients, stir well then spoon into the greased basin.

7   Using the back of a spoon press the pudding mixture evenly into the basin.

8   Stand the pudding on a microwave rack and cover with a plate or a piece of loosely fitting clingfilm which has been pierced two or three times. Pull the film to form a 'tent' above the basin.

9   Cook on HIGH for 3 minutes 30 seconds then MEDIUM for 12 minutes.

10 Leave to stand for 5 minutes then turn onto a serving plate.

Selections per serving:
   1 Bread
   1½ Fruit
   ¼ Protein
   30 Optional Calories

N.B. If making this pudding a day or two before it is to be served cook as above, leave to stand then turn out and check the pudding is thoroughly cooked. Place the basin over the pudding and leave until cool then wrap in greaseproof paper. To reheat: place the pudding on a serving plate and sprinkle over 1 tablespoon water. Cover with an inverted pudding basin and cook on HIGH for 4 minutes, leave for 2 minutes then serve.

Fruit Cake

Serves 12
275 Calories per serving

This fruit cake is suitable for a birthday or special occasion.

1lb (480g) dried mixed fruit

¾ pint (450ml) boiling water

3½oz (105g) margarine

3oz (90g) soft brown sugar

1 tablespoon treacle

2 large eggs (size 2), lightly beaten

¼ teaspoon gravy browning – optional

7oz (210g) self-raising flour, wholemeal or white

1 teaspoon mixed spice

1 teaspoon lemon juice

1½ tablespoons sieved apricot jam or conserve

1 tablespoon desiccated coconut

1   Place the fruit and water in a bowl, cover and cook on HIGH for 5 minutes. Leave for 30 minutes then drain and cool.

2   Line a 7½ inch (18.75cm) straight-sided dish with non-stick baking parchment.

3   Cream the margarine, sugar and treacle until light and fluffy. Gradually beat in about three-quarters of the egg and the gravy browning.

4   Sieve the flour and mixed spice into the creamed mixture, tip any bran remaining in the sieve into the bowl. Add the fruit, remaining egg and lemon juice. Carefully fold the ingredients together. Spoon the mixture into the prepared dish, level the surface make a slight dip in the centre.

5   Stand the container on a rack and cook on LOW for 25 minutes or until the top of the cake is almost dry and the sides have begun to shrink from the dish. Gently insert a cocktail stick into the centre of the cake. If cooked it will remain clean. Leave the cake in the dish for 6 minutes then turn out and remove the paper from the base. If the base is slightly damp, lay the cake upside down on the rack and cook on LOW for a short time until it is dry. Transfer to a wire rack and leave to cool.

6   When the cake is cool place the lemon juice and apricot jam in a small basin or cup and cook on HIGH for 30 seconds. Brush the warm glaze all over the top of the cake, then sprinkle with the coconut.

Selections per serving:
   ½ Bread
   1½ Fat
   1¼ Fruit
   75 Optional Calories

Small Fruit Cakes

Serves 9
105 Calories per serving

I find the small microwave poaching cups ideal for this recipe as they can be arranged in a circle. However, if you don't have any, use small ramekins or cups. Although it isn't normally advisable to remove the cakes from the dishes so soon after baking, I have found that they are less likely to have 'soggy bottoms' if transferred as soon as they are firm.

1½oz (45g) margarine

1½oz (45g) caster sugar

1 teaspoon golden syrup

gravy browning (optional)

1 egg, lightly beaten

2½oz (75g) self-raising flour, sieved

1oz (30g) mixed dried fruit

2 teaspoons water

Selections per serving:
  ¼ Bread
  1 Fat
  40 Optional Calories

1   Place a double thickness of cake cases in five poaching cups or a muffin pan.

2   Cream the margarine and sugar together until white and fluffy.

3   Beat in the golden syrup.

4   Mix a little gravy browning into the egg and gradually beat about half the egg into the creamed mixture.

5   Fold the flour, mixed fruit, remaining egg and water into the mixture.

6   Place heaped teaspoons of the mixture into the paper cases and cook on HIGH for 1 minute – 1 minute 10 seconds until the cakes are slightly moist on the top.

7   Remove from the oven and allow the cakes to cool a little then, using the edges of the paper cases, carefully lift the cakes out of the cooking dishes. Repeat the procedure to make four more cakes but reduce the cooking time by a few seconds.

Spicy Ring Cake

Serves 10
210 Calories per serving

If you don't have a ring mould make your own by placing a glass in a round dish, remembering to allow plenty of room for the cake to rise. The mixture must only half fill the dish.

3½oz (105g) margarine

3oz (90g) soft brown sugar

1 teaspoon golden syrup

3 eggs, lightly beaten

5oz (150g) self-raising wholemeal flour

½-¾ teaspoon allspice

2½oz (75g) sultanas

4 teaspoons water

1 teaspoon icing sugar

1 Remove 1 teaspoon margarine from the measured amount and grease a 2½ pint (1.8 litre) ring mould.

2 Cream the remaining margarine together with the sugar and syrup. Gradually beat in half the eggs. Stir in the remaining egg with the flour, allspice, sultanas and 4 teaspoons water to form a slack mixture which easily drops from the spoon. If necessary add a little more water.

3 Spoon the mixture into the greased ring mould and level the surface. Place the mould on a roasting trivet or an upturned plate in the oven.

4 Cook uncovered on MEDIUM for 4 minutes 30 seconds then increase the power to HIGH and cook for 2 minutes 30 seconds.

5 Remove the cake from the oven when the top is still moist and leave for 5-6 minutes. During this time the top should have set, if it is still wet return to the oven and cook for a few seconds. Allow the cake to cool for 10 minutes.

6 Lay a piece of non-stick baking parchment over a wire cooling rack, lay the rack over the ring mould, invert and lift off the mould. Leave until cold.

7 Transfer the cake to a serving plate and sieve the icing sugar through a fine sieve or tea strainer over the ring.

Selections per serving:
½ Bread
2 Fat
¼ Fruit
¼ Protein
50 Optional Calories

Sponge Cake

Serves 10
185 Calories per serving

A traditional sponge cake is baked in two halves but a much better result is obtained by baking a microwaved cake in one deep dish then cutting it in half.

3oz (90g) margarine

1½oz (45g) caster sugar

½ tablespoon golden syrup

2 large eggs, size 2, lightly beaten

few drops of vanilla essence

6oz (180g) self-raising flour

3-4 tablespoons water

4 tablespoons strawberry or raspberry jam

1 teaspoon icing sugar

1   Line the base and sides of a 7 inch (17.5cm) straight-sided dish with non-stick baking parchment.

2   Beat the margarine together with the sugar and golden syrup.

3   Beat about one third to half the eggs into the margarine mixture. Add the vanilla essence.

4   Sieve the flour and fold it with the water into the creamed mixture. The mixture should be slacker than a conventionally baked cake mixture and should drop from a spoon when very lightly shaken.

5   Spoon the mixture into the prepared dish and cook, uncovered, on MEDIUM for 2 minutes then on HIGH for 1 minute 40 seconds or until the sponge is still slightly damp. Leave to stand for 6-7 minutes by which time the top should look and feel firm when touched lightly with a finger. Leave to stand a further 1-2 minutes.

6   Lay a piece of non-stick baking parchment on a wire cooling rack and turn the cake out of the container, remove the paper and leave to cool on the wire rack.

7   When cold cut the sponge horizontally in half and spread with the jam. Sandwich the halves together then, using a sieve, sprinkle over the icing sugar. Store in an airtight tin.

Selections per serving:
    ½ Bread
    1¾ Fat
    65 Optional Calories

Spongy Buns

Serves 12
140 Calories per serving

Use the large juicy raisins for this recipe, the smaller variety tend to dry a little during cooking.

1½oz (45g) margarine

2oz (60g) soft brown sugar

1 tablespoon golden syrup

1 egg, lightly beaten

2½oz (75g) raisins

8oz (240g) plain flour (half wholemeal and half white or all white)

2½ teaspoons baking powder

¼ teaspoon mixed spice

6 tablespoons water

1 Cream the margarine together with the sugar and syrup. Gradually beat in the egg.

2 Stir the raisins into the creamed mixture.

3 Sieve the flour together with the baking powder and mixed spice, if using wholemeal flour tip the bran remaining in the sieve into the bowl.

4 Fold the flour and water into the creamed mixture. Mark the mixture into three, leave in the bowl.

5 Lay a piece of non-stick baking parchment on a microwave roasting rack and spoon a third of the mixture into four buns – do not smooth or level the surface of the mixture, leave in little heaps.

6 Cook on HIGH for 1 minute 30 seconds – 1 minute 40 seconds until firm when gently touched but still damp. Remove the roasting rack from the oven and slide the non-stick baking parchment onto a wire cooling rack.

7 Cover the roasting rack with a second piece of non-stick baking parchment and continue with the next third of mixture until it has all been cooked. Leave the buns to cool a little but when sufficiently firm remove from the baking parchment and leave to cool on the wire rack.

Selections per serving:
½ Bread
¾ Fat
60 Optional Calories

Pastry Flan Case

Makes an 8 inch (20cm) round flan case to serve 8
135 Calories per serving

Shortcrust pastry baked in the microwave must be rolled thinner than usual as there is no dry heat and if too thick the centre of the pastry case remains soggy. As soon as the pastry case is cool enough to handle remove it from the flan dish and place on a cooling rack, this too will help to prevent a soggy base.

5oz (150g) plain flour, plus 2 teaspoons

pinch of salt

2½oz (75g) margarine

1½-2 tablespoons ice cold water

1 Line the base of an 8 inch (20cm) flan dish with a circle of non-stick baking parchment.

2 Sieve the flour and salt into a bowl, add the margarine, if possible margarine which has been stored in the freezer. Rub into the flour until the mixture resembles fresh breadcrumbs.

3 Mix the cold water into the pastry with a round-bladed knife. If time allows, wrap in greaseproof paper and refrigerate for 15-20 minutes.

4 Dust the work surface with the remaining flour. Roll out the pastry using short, light movements away from you.

5 Fold the pastry circle loosely into quarters then transfer to the flan dish, unfold and gently press into the dish. Trim any overhanging pastry. Chill for 20-30 minutes.

6 Use a fork to prick the base and sides of the flan. Transfer the dish to the oven and stand on a microwave rack or an upturned plate. Cook on HIGH for 5 minutes or until the centre of the flan looks dry. Remove the flan dish from the oven and leave to stand for 4 minutes. As soon as the flan is cool enough to handle turn out of the dish, remove the non-stick paper and transfer to a cooling rack.

Selections per serving:
½ Bread
1½ Fat
30 Optional Calories

Questions and Answers

Q. Is it safe to buy a second-hand oven?

A. Only if it has been checked by a qualified engineer.

Q. What will happen if the oven is switched on without anything in the chamber?

A. It could damage the magnetron. It's a good idea to leave a cup of water in the chamber to prevent accidents.

Q. Why doesn't food brown during cooking?

A. Some foods do brown if high in sugar or fat. Beef browns during roasting as the fat becomes hot, nuts brown due to their high fat content and syrups brown and can burn as they attract microwaves. The majority of foods do not brown as there is no dry heat in a microwave.

Q. Why should food be covered during cooking?

A. The covering prevents moisture escaping and stops the food drying out.

Q. Why should food be stirred or rearranged during cooking?

A. To aid even cooking.

Q. Does the size and shape of the cooking container influence cooking?

A. Yes, high sided dishes and those with corners or very sloping sides affect cooking. High sided dishes shield the microwaves and square and rectangular dishes overcook at the corners.

Q. Why shouldn't salt be added to food before cooking?

A. Salt draws the moisture from the food causing it to dry out. Occasionally salt is included, for example it can be added to the water when cooking pasta.

Q. Why is the standing time important?

A. Food continues to cook even when it is no longer in the microwave. This is not due to any microwave activity, it is the conduction of heat within the food.

Questions and Answers

Q. Why do different foods of the same weight require different cooking times?

A. The density of food as well as its weight and composition affect cooking. Microwaves cannot penetrate dense food, such as meat, as quickly as the same weight of bread which has a more open texture.

Q. Do all frozen foods have to be thawed before cooking?

A. No, but always check the instructions on pre-frozen foods. Remember the starting temperature of food will affect its cooking time.

Q. Is it safe to use aluminium cooking foil in the microwave?

A. Always check the microwave's instruction manual. Usually small pieces of smooth foil can safely be used but foil must never touch any part of the oven.

Q. Can plastic containers be used in the microwave?

A. Some plastics are ideal for microwave cooking. These include the thin semi-disposable microwave-safe containers such as ring moulds and cake dishes. Rigid hard plastics called thermoplastics can be used in the microwave, in the conventional oven, and for freezing. However, always refer to the manufacturer's instructions as most plastic containers which are ideal for storing food, like yogurt containers and plastic bags are not suitable.

Q. Is it safe to use clingfilm in the microwave?

A. Ordinary clingfilm should never be used for microwave cooking and recent guidelines from the Ministry of Agriculture advise restricted use of 'microwave-safe' film. It is considered safe to use the microwave film for covering food but the food should not be in direct contact with it. Therefore only use the film to cover food which is in a bowl or on a lipped plate. Do not wrap food in it.

Q. What happens if the oven door is opened while something is cooking in the microwave?

A. The power automatically cuts off and, as long as the door is only opened for a short time, cooking will not be impaired. Cake mixtures, for example, will collapse when the power is cut off but as soon as the door is closed and the power resumes the mixture will rise once again.

INDEX